M000113898

Prayers of Blessing Over My Marriage

BRUCE WILKINSON

and HEATHER HAIR

HARVEST HOUSE PUBLISHERS
EUGENE, OREGON

Prayers of Blessing over My Marriage
Copyright © 2019 by Bruce Wilkinson and Heather Hair
Published by Harvest House Publishers
Eugene, Oregon 97408
www.harvesthousepublishers.com

ISBN 978-0-7369-7185-0 (pbk.)
ISBN 978-0-7369-7186-7 (eBook)

Library of Congress Cataloging-in-Publication Data is on file at the Library of Congress, Washington, DC.

Printed in the United States of America

18 19 20 21 22 23 24 25 26 27 / VP-RD / 10 9 8 7 6 5 4 3 2 1

*Each author would like to lovingly dedicate
this book to their spouse—*

from Bruce to Darlene

from Heather to Jack

Gratitude and prayers surround you both, always.

Contents

Note to the Reader

Praying for your marriage is one of the most important things you can do. Praying together as a couple for your marriage is even better. Your marriage has been given to you by God as a gift and a tool to enable both of you to fully live out His purpose for your lives. You are to be teammates, romantic partners, and friends. Life's journey has many ups and downs, and facing these together as a couple will enable you to navigate them far better than you could on your own.

You'll find each of the following 20 prayer subjects divided into five parts. We begin with Scripture to reflect on. Next, we follow that with a section called "Preparing Our Hearts"—some devotional thoughts aimed at guiding your heart and mind into alignment with God's Word and a spirit of prayer. Lastly, we have chosen to model the three parts of the prayer portion off of a pattern for prayer found in 2 Chronicles 20:6-12. This includes:

Praising God
(2 Chronicles 20:6-9)

Lord, the God of our ancestors, are you not the God who is in heaven? You rule over all the kingdoms of the nations. Power and might are in your hand, and no one can withstand you. Our God, did you not drive out the inhabitants of this land before your people Israel and give it forever to the descendants of Abraham your friend? They have lived in it and have built in it a sanctuary for your Name, saying, "If calamity comes upon us, whether the sword of judgment, or plague or famine, we will stand in your presence before this temple that bears your Name and will cry out to you in our distress, and you will hear us and save us."

Presenting the Situation
(2 Chronicles 20:10-11)

But now here are men from Ammon, Moab and Mount Seir, whose territory you would not allow Israel to invade when they came from Egypt; so they turned away from them and did not destroy them. See how they are repaying us by coming to drive us out of the possession you gave us as an inheritance.

Prayer for Blessing and Freedom
(2 Chronicles 20:12)

Our God, will you not judge them? For we have no power to face this vast army that is attacking us. We do not know what to do, but our eyes are on you.

This is not a magical pattern meant to make all your prayers come true. But it is an established pattern in Scripture for how to approach the throne of God and talk to Him about your needs. Remember, the main thing in having your prayers answered is found in your abiding relationship with Jesus Christ. But this pattern serves as a structure we've used in guiding married couples around the world through the process of zeroing in on more specific, regular, and affirming prayers for their relationship.

We pray as your prayer journey continues to develop more fully that God Himself will bless you indeed. We pray that He will place His hand upon you and expand the borders of your marital influence. We also pray that He will keep you from pain while He provides you with a supernatural covering.

May you pray regularly, fervently, and with great expectations!

—Bruce Wilkinson

1

Christ

*For no one can lay any foundation other than
the one already laid, which is Jesus Christ.*

1 CORINTHIANS 3:11

Preparing Our Hearts

The foundation of any marriage is Jesus Christ. He is
to be the centrality of focus, the source of hope, the stabilizer in struggles, and the impetus for righteous living. Lead
with Christ as a couple, and you will have all that you need
for every situation you face. But what does it mean to lead
with Christ or to make Him the foundation? Many couples give verbal assent to this but fail to carry it out in application. Verbal assent will not accomplish all you need it to
do. Jesus Himself said that there are many in this world
who call on His name but do not know Him, and He likewise does not know them in a relational, intimate manner
(Matthew 7:21-23).

Making Christ the center of your marriage involves a
consistent abiding in His presence, surrender to His Lord-
ship, attentiveness to His words, and reflection of His character. Leaving even one of those areas out is like removing

11

THE FOUNDATION OF
ANY MARRIAGE IS
Jesus Christ.
HE IS TO BE THE CENTRALITY
OF FOCUS, THE SOURCE
OF HOPE, THE STABILIZER
IN STRUGGLES,
AND THE IMPETUS
FOR RIGHTEOUS LIVING.

a leg from a chair while still expecting it to stand upright. Without each leg in place, the chair will topple.

Jesus is not a cross to be hung on the wall of your home or stuck in the yard with a stake. He's not even just a name to tag on to the end of your prayers. While those reminders are nice and reflective, they alone are not enough for your marriage to receive the full benefits of Christ (John 10:10). It is in your ongoing attachment to Jesus that you will discover His power in your home (John 15).

Consider your marriage relationship for a moment in comparison to what it means to abide in Christ. If you or your spouse only acknowledged each other's presence before a meal or when you needed something, how do you think that would bode on the level of your intimacy? What if the only words you or your spouse brought to the other were complaints or requests, and even those came sporadically? Or if you listed off the things for which you were grateful practically by rote, while your eyes dulled and you drifted off to sleep?

Consider if your spouse asked you out on a date and you said you didn't have time but that you'd meet with them for five minutes at the start of every day to read something together. That way, at least, you could check off your "time together" and know you did your part. Would your spouse prefer dinner with you on a date or five minutes in the morning?

If we treated the abiding aspect of our marriage like so many of us treat the abiding aspect of our relationship with Jesus Christ, our marriages would suffer under the strain of distance, isolation, and demand. Jesus loves you with a love like no other. He cares about what you are thinking, where you are going, and what you are dreaming. He wants to know that you took notice of His creation or provision or presence, just like you desire your spouse to take notice of you and what you wear or how you look. We are made in the image of God, thus these same emotions which long for connection, attention, and love have been placed inside of us because they resemble the emotions of the One who created us. Abiding in Christ as a couple requires an intentional mindset of inclusion, deference, and gratitude toward and with the One who loves you most. It isn't something to do that you can just check off a list. If your spouse put a list in the kitchen of all the things you should do in order to receive his or her approval, it would be frowned upon. Jesus is not withholding His approval waiting for you to open your Bible app or say a quick prayer. He desires you—the both of you— to faithfully walk with Him in the enjoyment and instruction of His presence.

Praising God

Heavenly Father, thank You for the gift of Your Son, Jesus Christ, and all that He has provided for us through His death, burial, and resurrection. Thank You for opening the pathway to You through Him so that we might have the opportunity for closeness with You. I praise You for the spiritual blessings You've chosen to give to my spouse and me. I thank You that You have a plan for our lives, and it is a good plan filled with a future and with hope. I honor You for enabling these things to even take place by virtue of Christ's sacrifice for sin. Help me not to neglect so great a salvation or so awesome a gift. Help us as a couple to continually live with a heart of gratitude and praise for who You are and what You have allowed us to experience in Christ.

Presenting the Situation

Use this portion to give some time toward thinking about your abiding relationship with Christ. Consider it for yourself as an individual, but also consider your conversations as a couple, your shared prayer times together, and your focus. When issues arise, is Christ brought into the equation? When blessings occur, is He acknowledged first and foremost? Is the time you spend in the Word more focused on looking for an answer or crossing off a list than it is on exploring the mind of Christ? Reflect on these questions, and consider some of your own which will help you to identify ways you and your spouse can include Jesus Christ as a regular part of your lives.

Prayer for Blessing and Freedom

Gracious Lord, You represent and reflect the true image of love. The love of Jesus Christ is patient, kind, merciful, never boasting, forgiving, forbearing, gentle, and always present. As we grow closer to Jesus in our hearts and our minds, we will reflect this love in our marriage and to those around us. Remind us of Your presence. Open our eyes to see and identify You in our lives. Let our conversations involve You more than they already do, and help our thoughts to remain on and in You. Delight us with Your desires, Jesus, as You reveal to us the pleasures of abiding in You in our lives and in our marriage. In Your name, amen.

Spiritual Growth

*But grow in the grace and knowledge of
our Lord and Savior Jesus Christ. To him
be glory both now and forever! Amen.*

2 PETER 3:18

Preparing Our Hearts

If you've ever watched a child learn gymnastics, I'm sure
you've seen your fill of mishaps. No one starts out in the
sport by completing a backflip or walking steadily across a
balance beam. Each week moms and dads take their children to gymnastics lessons because to master the skills in the
sport, practice is necessary.

What would happen if a parent brought their child to
the first gymnastics lesson and expected little junior to be an
Olympic star from the start? Most people would think that
this parent had lost his or her mind. But even though we all
know that progression in a sport requires time, effort, and
dedication, very few of us realize that our spiritual development requires nothing less. You don't become wise, patient,
discerning, steady, unconditionally loving, and everything
else that a spiritually mature person embodies the moment
you get saved. Rather, Peter reminds us where we all start

GROWING SPIRITUALLY

as a couple

PROVIDES YOU WITH

THE FOUNDATION

YOU NEED

TO MAXIMIZE

the full experience

OF YOUR RELATIONSHIP.

out on this journey: as babies. He writes in 1 Peter 2:2, "Like newborn babies, crave pure spiritual milk, so that by it you may grow up in your salvation…"

Why is growing spiritually so important to a marriage relationship? Growing spiritually as a couple provides you with the foundation you need to maximize the full experience of your relationship. Much of the conflict that couples face stems from a lack of spiritual and/or emotional maturity. But growing spiritually as a couple doesn't happen just because you are saved, or even because you attend church or a small group. Growing spiritually results from ongoing exposure to, study of, and application of God's Word (Matthew 18:20; John 8:31). It also results from a continual abiding in Christ Himself (John 15).

Be diligent to encourage each other and pray for each other regarding this area of spiritual growth. It's been placed at the very start of this prayer guide due to its importance. As you grow in Christ and become transformed and renewed in your minds through the power of the Holy Spirit, you will discover strength, contentment, joy, and peace in your marriage like never before.

Just like a small child must practice cartwheel after cartwheel after cartwheel before they become second nature and can be performed well, married couples must routinely exercise and develop their spiritual insights and muscles in order to fully and freely live in the art of mutual grace.

Praising God

Heavenly Father, You desire that we grow in both Your grace and in our understanding and knowledge of who You are. In doing so, we become transformed into the image of Christ (Romans 8:29). We also discover in the process of trusting that You work all things out for those who are called according to Your purpose and for Your glory (Romans 8:28). We praise You that You have made Yourself available to us so that we can grow in our relationship with You. The universe and all of creation is Yours and yet You desire that we know You in a personal way. Thank You for awakening in each of us a desire to know You more deeply and providing the pathway through Your Son, Jesus Christ, to You so that we may know You and grow in the grace You have supplied.

Presenting the Situation

Use this portion of your prayer to the Lord to share with Him about your specific situation related to spiritual growth as a couple. Whether you desire greater attentiveness toward this in your spouse or in yourself, or whether you are looking for more effective ways to grow spiritually—give these concerns to God in prayer. Pray about the things that God has placed on your heart in this area of life. It may be about how to set aside dedicated time for devotions or Scripture reading as a couple. Or it may be about how to be more consistent in attending church. Whatever it is, write out or simply pray about the unique aspects of spiritual growth that are present in your marriage at the moment, then watch the Lord answer these prayers. Record the answers to your prayers in the margins or in the room provided when they occur.

_____

_____

_____

Prayer for Blessing and Freedom

Gracious Lord, open the eyes of our hearts in order to recognize Your grace in our lives. Encourage conversations between us as a couple that reflect on Your movement and intervention in our lives. Motivate us to spend time together with You in ways that develop us spiritually. Give us wisdom concerning what to focus on that will help us to grow in our relationship with You on a deeper level. Show us ways in which we can encourage each other to grow spiritually, and help that encouragement to come across as authentic and not as nagging or criticizing. Cultivate our spirits so that we are open to the seed of Your Word. In Christ's name, amen.

3

Compassion

Instead, we were like young children among you.
Just as a nursing mother cares for her children.

1 THESSALONIANS 2:7

Preparing Our Hearts

When two people live as closely together as the marriage relationship entails, a natural crisscrossing of emotional needs occurs. When one spouse struggles, the other may feel and reflect that struggle internally. When one spouse lacks energy, the other may pick up on that and take the burden upon themselves. We aren't always aware of the causes and effects that run through the gamut of our marital emotional cadence. But practicing an intention of compassionate mindfulness will heighten this awareness and create an increase in mutual care.

In the busy state in which our lives often reside, intentional awareness toward our internal fluctuations takes practice. It also takes prayer. It requires thinking outside of our own egos and beyond the next activity on our list. But it is possible when you commit yourselves to cherishing your spouse more greatly through the gift of compassion.

Author and philosopher Leo Buscaglia once spoke

about a contest he had been asked to judge. The judges were tasked with the daunting role of identifying and naming the most compassionate child who had entered the contest. Out of all of the many activities, words, and caring expressions the judges had to choose from, they landed on a young boy whose winning actions may surprise you.

When his elderly neighbor lost his wife to illness, the young boy walked over to his house, climbed up into his lap, and sat there. Like Jesus weeping with Mary and Martha rather than relying on logic or language to explain that Lazarus had really just gone on to heaven and that heaven was actually great, the boy—relying on the wisdom of childlike intuition—simply let a tear or two fall as well. Later, when his mom asked what he had said to help lift the spirit of the elderly neighbor, her son replied, "Nothing. I just helped him cry."

Similarly, compassion in a marriage relationship often comes clothed in quiet. A hand held. A tear wiped. Or even a tear shared. It's found in giving space when space is needed. Prayer when words won't work. Compassion calls for withholding judgment, reducing what may feel like "personally urgent" demands or requests, and setting the other's spiritual and emotional needs in front of our own in that moment.

Compassion calls for quiet. It is within this gift of stillness and silence that you validate the sting. You don't try to fix it. You don't try to wipe it away. You simply allow it, and in allowing it, you soothe it.

If only we lived in a world where every spouse was as wise as this contest-winning four-year-old boy. If we did, we would see many more satisfying marriages than we do now.

COMPASSION IN A

marriage relationship

OFTEN COMES CLOTHED

IN QUIET.

A HAND HELD.

A TEAR WIPED.

OR EVEN

A TEAR SHARED.

Healed marriages. Happy marriages. Uplifted. Understood. We would also hear a lot less complaining while experiencing a lot more embracing. Who knows—we might even usher in some of our own Lazarus-level resurrections as well. Resurrections of dreams, hopes, hearts, and homes. Compassion goes a long way, like the calming effect of the breeze on a hot day.

Praising God

Heavenly Father, You embody the spirit of compassion. Time and again, You have shown this compassion to those You call Your own. When Jesus walked on earth, He was filled with compassion for those who followed Him, seeing them as sheep without a shepherd (Matthew 9:36). It was His compassion that caused Him to weep at the experience of Martha and Mary's pain in the face of their brother's death, even though He Himself knew that death was simply a passage into eternity (John 11:35). Compassion isn't sympathy. Compassion goes deeper than sympathy. It is a grace for another's pain even if that pain isn't understood or felt personally. We praise You for the compassion that You have shown in our lives and in the lives of those who seek You. This compassion, at its greatest level, provided Jesus Christ as our Savior so that we could be saved from eternal separation from you (John 3:16). Thank You for honoring the humble state of our hearts through Your compassion and modeling that for us in such a way that we are to reflect it to others.

Presenting the Situation

Use this portion to bring specific concerns, circumstances, or challenges your marriage may be facing due to a lack of compassion or a lack of expressing that compassion to each other. This may include ways in which you speak to each other as a couple, or how you address each other's needs or pains in life, whether they are current or from the past. If there is an area where you do not feel that your spouse understands certain pain you have, ask God to open up their heart to feel and show compassion even without having to understand the pain itself. Pray also for yourself to recognize needs in your spouse which can benefit from your own compassionate response. Write these out as the Lord brings them to mind, and be attentive to express your love with gentleness and compassion.

Prayer for Blessing and Freedom

Gracious Lord, I desire a deeper level of compassion between my spouse and me. It is easy to take each other for granted and overlook hurts, disappointments, or fears the other is facing. Enlarge our level of care for each other in such a way that gentleness and a spirit of compassion become the norm between us. The world provides little respite from the pains of life. You have brought us together as vessels of love for each other. Keep us from the temptations of distraction so that we are present with each other and our moments are comprised of compassion. When we do not live up to the expectation of the other, help us not to jump to conclusions or blame out of our own frustration or pain, but rather to develop a skill in communication that gives us the ability to discover what may have contributed to the situation or unmet expectation. Help us to see from the other's perspective and to always show grace while giving the benefit of the doubt. Give us the strength and wisdom to resist the urge to try and "fix" whatever is bothering our spouse at the moment. Keep us from thoughts which focus on our own selfish needs or desires to just move past the pain so we can get on with life or life's lists. Help us, instead, to give the space needed and the presence needed for our spouse to feel our compassion and to benefit from it. In Christ's name, amen.

4

Focus

Set your minds on things above, not on earthly things.

COLOSSIANS 3:2

Preparing Our Hearts

There existed a time when the only way to get professional-looking photographs required hiring a professional photographer. Family portraits took place once a year, if that. Families often waited until the local church brought in a photographer for the church's membership catalog. Then time slots were chosen, outfits were purchased, and families made their way to pose for the camera. A few weeks later, the photographer placed different package options in front of each family to be considered and chosen for purchase. Purchase at a pretty steep price, mind you.

Today, however, professional-looking photographs often require little more than your or a friend's smartphone. The resolution quality, along with the camera's preprogrammed abilities to isolate the position of focus, can make the average person's pictures look like portraits. In fact, one smartphone even offers "portrait" mode to give the additional effect of blurring the background while sharpening the person or object of choice.

Focus matters.

What the professional photographer understood to do with the various buttons, lenses, and lighting options necessary to operate the equipment from days gone by, smartphones now enable pretty much everyone to do simply by aiming in the right direction.

The ease of this focus has allowed families to have portraits made much more frequently than before, not to mention much more cheaply. It's allowed for not just a roll of film, or two rolls, to capture a vacation, but rather hundreds, if not thousands, of photos to catch and share these memories. It's also allowed parents to have more than the yearly portrait of the littles as they grow, but rather a daily timeline of growth, joys, activities, and sweet sayings caught on film. Yes, live photos now add video and audio to a photo as well. This enables all of us to seize segments of our seconds at random, simply for our sentimental remembrance.

The bottom line: We're able to do more when we're able to focus well.

Our spiritual lives reflect this reality too. When we are weighed down with the cumbersome need to control everything ourselves—adjust every angle, move every light, lift every chin, pose every moment—we miss out on the ability to do much at all. We spend the bulk of our time dictating our distractions instead of dwelling in our destinies. We willingly enslave ourselves to the tyranny of the urgent. We forget the value of a moment, a word, a look, a hug, or even a shared meal. Our marriages fall prey to frenzy rather than

If you long for
MORE SPECIAL MOMENTS,

MORE PEACE,

MORE MEMORIES

in your marriage,
FOCUS ON GOD.

peace. But God tells us that when we focus on Him, peace presides. "You will keep in perfect peace all who trust in you, all whose thoughts are fixed on you" (Isaiah 26:3 NLT).

If you long for more special moments, more peace, more memories in your marriage, focus on God. Let Him figure out the details and blur out the backgrounds. When you do, you will discover the tremendous beauty right before your very eyes.

Praising God

Heavenly Father, You are seated above all and Your rule is carried out over all (Psalm 115:3). We honor Your position as supreme authority. Through Christ, the world was created, and in Christ all things are held together (Colossians 1:16). You hold things in place, and by Your plans, a matter is established. We give You praise and thanksgiving for the power which is Yours, knowing that it is this power which enables us to live out our days. It is Your divine wisdom and authority which have positioned us on earth to carry out the plans You have for us. And in Your wisdom, You have brought us together as a couple, knowing that we can accomplish more for Your glory in this way. We praise You for Your great might and for Your victory over our enemy, Satan, and his demons (Colossians 2:15). It is in that victory where we find our own confidence to live, work, and move forward in the purposes for which You have called us. It is in Your love that we are able to know what it means to cherish the love of each other. When our eyes are on You, we are set free to experience and enjoy the gifts and grace found within our spouse. We are set free to overlook unmet expectations as we rest in the knowledge of Your control and providential mercies.

Presenting the Situation

Use this portion to direct your thoughts to specific areas in your marriage where distractions or worries may interfere with the confident peace and assurance which comes from faith in God. You may want to spend time writing out a diary of how you and your spouse spend your time and on what you focus your thoughts. Then take a moment to place these before God in prayer, asking Him for wisdom about which things remove your focus from what He has for you to do or to be. Sometimes the things Satan uses to distract us do not seem overtly evil and so we maintain their presence in our lives longer than we should. But anything that siphons your attention off of God's presence and purpose for you as a couple should be examined as to its true worth.

Prayer for Blessing and Freedom

Gracious Lord, life has a way of interfering in our thoughts and our focus, distracting us from what matters most. We come before You as a couple and pray that, in our marriage, You will help us to stay focused on You and Your values and Your calling for our lives. Part of that focus is in living out our relationship together, embodying the character of Christ to each other. Help us to stay attentive to the need for this character in how we address each other and serve each other. Another part of that focus entails facing spiritual warfare from the perspective of victory rather than defeat, knowing that You are seated in the heavenlies, above all rule, power, and authority, and that through Jesus Christ's death and resurrection, we are also seated with You. Give us insight and wisdom on the decisions we make as a couple that will reflect a long-term, eternal focus, rather than a short-term, material mindset. And reveal to us throughout the moments of our days the blessing and peace that come through keeping our thoughts set on You. When our focus centers on You, worry and anxiety cannot keep us from embracing our relationship fully. Set us free to fully live out the blessings of our marriage by keeping our focus on You and the wisdom, comfort, and assurances we find in Your truth. In Christ's name, amen.

5

Favor

May the favor of the Lord our God rest on us; establish the work of our hands for us— yes, establish the work of our hands.

PSALM 90:17

Preparing Our Hearts

"Will you do me a favor?" It's a question we either get asked or ask of someone else. We call in a favor from someone when we need them to do something for us that goes beyond the normal or expected behaviors of life. Favors might include something as small as having a family member bring you a drink from the kitchen as you watch your most-loved television show. Or it could be something as significant as having a former boss give a call on your behalf to the place where you are applying. Or posting a recommendation of you on your professional profile.

Favors require extra effort from someone else in order to provide us with something more at the moment. In fact, one business took the concept full force when they named themselves "Favor" and set up a system where people will shop for you, run errands for you, or simply water your flowers when you don't feel like doing it yourself. For a fee,

God's favor comes
WRAPPED IN GRACE
AND TIED WITH THE
BOW OF BLESSING.
WHAT'S MORE,
Scripture tells us
THAT GOD'S FAVOR
WON'T FADE UPON DELIVERY
OR BE USED UP
BY ASKING TOO MUCH.

you can log onto the app, and willing individuals are waiting to do your favor. If they do great, you give them a sizable tip.

Favors come in all shapes and sizes, but regardless of how they come, they are always appreciated simply because they are more than what we are entitled to receive from anyone at any time.

Did you know that God does favors too? His favors come wrapped in grace and tied with the bow of blessing. What's more, Scripture tells us that God's favor won't fade upon delivery or be used up by asking too much. Rather, we are told in Psalm 30:5 that God's favor lasts a lifetime.

Favor over your marriage can open the doors to peace, greater enjoyment, and a deeper level of contentment than you've ever known. This is because with God's favor come all good things (Psalm 84:11), protection (Psalm 5:12), and opportunity (Genesis 39:4). As you discover new ways of ushering in the abundance of favor into your marriage and into your home, you will feel the impact of ease, power, and grace.

So, how do you get favor? It's simple. You ask for it. Just like you'd ask a friend or family member to do you a favor, asking God to give you His favor kick-starts the process of receiving. Take Nehemiah, for example. If you've ever read through the book in the Bible named after him, you'll see a repeated phrase occurring. It's Nehemiah asking God to give him favor. Nehemiah 5:19 is an example: "Remember me with favor, my God, for all I have done for these people."

Another important aspect of seeking God's favor shows up in the verse we just read. Nehemiah based his request for God's favor on the goodness he had already done for God's people. This is similar to how we often trade favors with others we know. If someone does you a really big favor, a common response is, "Thanks, I owe you one." Meaning that the next time that person needs a big favor, you are going to remember what they did for you, and that will serve as the catalyst for what you do for them. This is how Nehemiah sought God's favor in his prayers. Essentially, he reminded God of the sacrificial good he had done for God's people, and off of that asked that God would give him favor in the situation he was currently facing.

Incorporating intentional acts of service to others as a couple sets the foundation for your prayers of seeking God's favor in your marriage. God loves to bestow favor on His own. Don't be shy to ask Him for it, and then watch Him open the doors of opportunity, blessing, peace, and provision in your lives and in your marriage relationship.

Praising God

Heavenly Father, thank You for the favor You have shown us by sending Your Son, Jesus Christ, to offer His life as a sacrifice for our sins. It is only because of Your favor that we are able to pray to You in the first place. Favor provided forgiveness and opened the pathway for us to receive the gift of life, marriage, and fulfillment in any capacity at all. We give You praise for Your willingness to pour out Your favor on all who are undeserving, including ourselves. We honor Your name and thank You for the favor You have already shown us in bringing us together as a couple and enabling us to get married. We bless Your name, Lord, and offer You the truest expression of our heartfelt praise and gratitude.

Presenting the Situation

Use this portion to pray for anything in your marriage or home life that feels blocked, trapped, or isolated. Oftentimes, Satan will seek to distract our focus from God by placing obstacles in our paths. In this way, our thoughts become consumed with how to overcome the obstacles rather than with praising and thanking God in all things as we have been instructed (Philippians 4:6). God's favor can power through any issues you are facing relationally, and it can also open the doors to allow in unanticipated levels of blessing and grace. Go ahead and write down the dreams God has placed in your heart related to your marriage and your family. Then take time to ask God to give you His favor regarding these things. Keep track as the answers to your requests are provided so that you will be faithful to thank Him as He does give you His favor.

_____

_____

_____

_____

_____

Prayer for Blessing and Freedom

Gracious Lord, You have planted within us dreams and hopes wherein we seek to bring good to each other in our marriage and in our home and to those around us. The gifts and skills You've given us have come to us with a purpose in mind. Yet, so much can stand in the way of us living out the full expression of our destiny. It is Your favor which opens the doors and provides the clear path to a life of significance, satisfaction, and service. Pour out Your favor onto us as a couple, fueling us with peace, desire, and attraction for each other. Remember us for the good we have already done in Your name, and return upon us the favor we have sought to show others. Bless our hearts with the favor of Your love, letting it spill over into our emotions for each other. Teach us how to receive Your favor, to walk in it, and to make the practice of asking for it a continual process, filled with joyful expectations. In Christ's name, amen.

6

Peace

*Let the peace of Christ rule in your hearts,
since as members of one body you were
called to peace. And be thankful.*

<small>COLOSSIANS 3:15</small>

Preparing Our Hearts

As a child, I (Heather) flew often. My father was an airline captain for a major commercial airline, so flying was a normal mode of transportation. Some of my fondest memories include those afternoons where he flew me up with him on a trip when he was working, and we attended a sporting event or visited a museum during his layover. As you might imagine, with a lot of flying comes an increased opportunity for turbulence to occur. And I admit, despite countless hours in the air, I never got used to the turbulence.

But one thing would set me at ease no matter how bumpy a flight got: my father's words.

If my dad was in the cockpit and knew that we were coming up on some turbulence, he would make his way back to where I was, tell me to buckle up, and then say, "It's just like a roller coaster, Heather. It makes it more fun this way." He'd pause and then throw in a bit more for good measure: "I sure do get bored if it's just a smooth flight. How about you?"

I would always force a smile back at him and try to look brave as my knuckles started to turn white grasping both sides of my seat. But then, after he left to go back to the cockpit and fly, I'd rehearse my father's words over and over in my mind: "It's just like a roller coaster, Heather. It makes it more fun this way." And I'd remember the calm in his voice and on his face. A few minutes into the turbulence, and I'd have peace. Why? Because my dad had peace, and he was the one who was flying.

Now, I'll admit, when I fly today as an adult and we face some turbulence, I often hear his words but also realize he's not the one flying. So my heart starts racing, and my knuckles turn white as I squeeze my husband's hand or leg a bit too hard. But whenever my dad was the pilot, I flew in perfect peace regardless of the bumps. This is because I trusted him, no matter what.

God also gives us a promise of peace when we choose to trust Him rather than fear the circumstances that cause bumps in our marriage. Isaiah 26:3 tells us clearly, "You will keep in perfect peace those whose minds are steadfast, because they trust in you."

Marriage comes with some turbulence, no doubt. It's part of the process of pairing up two sinful human beings. Just like bumpy air is bound to happen if you fly long enough. God never promised us that the bumps would go away, just like my dad never promised me a smooth flight. But what God does do is give us the assurance that He is the One in control—He's the Captain of our lives, and He knows how to get us where we need to go.

In hindsight, now that I'm grown, I don't think my dad actually got bored on smooth flights or thought that turbulence was more fun. But when I was a child, he framed my experience in such a way that it gave me the opportunity to choose peace. Jesus has done something similar for us, painting life's difficulties in a way we can understand when He says, "I have told you these things, so that in me you may have peace. In this world you will have trouble. But take heart! I have overcome the world" (John 16:33). Truth is, He has overcome the world as a warrior battling fiercely against an enemy bent on our destruction. But Jesus doesn't go into those graphic details in this verse, just like my dad didn't tell me how bad the storms he was about to navigate both through and around actually were. Rather, Jesus simply reminds us to take heart by trusting Him. He reminds us that He has overcome. He smiles. Then He returns to battle on our behalf. Peace has been offered to us if we simply choose to believe Him and receive it.

Praising God

Heavenly Father, we praise You for all that You have gone through in order to secure our peace. We honor You for Your strength, knowledge, and ability to overcome the evil one. You know how to steer us through life's storms in such a way that brings us to the other side without harm. It is because of Your power that we can rest in peace. Give us greater insight into Your love and might so that we may have an increased level of peace. Let us see the calm of Your smile so that in it we can find serenity. You are the victorious warrior under whose wings we find refuge. Thank You for blessing us with Your presence and peace.

WHATEVER IT IS
that is disrupting
THE LEVEL OF PEACE

BETWEEN YOU

AND YOUR SPOUSE

AND WITHIN YOUR FAMILY,

ask God to intervene

AND PROVIDE YOU

WITH INSIGHT INTO

HIS POWER OVER IT ALL.

Presenting the Situation

Use this portion to identify areas in your marriage or home where chaos or difficulties abound. Take some time to write down specific things, whether it's how you communicate with each other, financial strains, health issues, problems with work, or situations with the children.

Whatever it is that is disrupting the level of peace between you and your spouse and within your family, ask God to intervene and provide you with insight into His power over it all. Ask Him to adjust your thinking in such a way that provides you with the ability to recognize that He is in control. Release your fears and anxieties to Him while you seek to trust His hand and His heart in every area of your life.

_____

_____

_____

_____

_____

Prayer for Blessing and Freedom

Gracious Lord, there are so many things which can elevate stress levels in our marriage and in our home. Things such as financial strain, work stress, family dynamics, health issues, and more can lead to worry or anxiety. When worry or anxiety increase, it becomes difficult for us as a couple to live freely within the blessings You've provided us. Rather than express our love to each other, we spend time analyzing issues or holding back emotions so that we have enough to go around. But, Lord, You are in charge. You are over all. You have overcome. And if we will focus our hearts and our minds on You, we can let go of that which worries us. We can experience Your peace that passes understanding. Speak to us in a way that we can hear You. Give us the gift of peace in our marriage. Let arguments and conflict be a thing of the past and not of the present. Rather, let peace rule our hearts in Christ Jesus. Show us what it means to truly know peace in our marriage, and deliver us from the bonds of fear. We trust You and thank You for all You have done and are doing. In Christ's name, amen.

7

Blessing

*Jabez cried out to the God of Israel, "Oh, that you
would bless me and enlarge my territory! Let your
hand be with me, and keep me from harm so that I
will be free from pain." And God granted his request.*

1 Chronicles 4:10

Preparing Our Hearts

A young boy went to the local shop on Main Street with
his mom one day while doing errands. They knew the shop
owner by name, and he greeted both of them when they
entered. His mom picked up the few items she needed and
was ready to check out when the shop owner looked down
at the young boy and then held out a jar of individually
wrapped Starbursts. "Grab you a handful," the shop owner
offered. The young boy looked at the jar of candy and then
put his hands in his pockets.

Assuming he had a sudden bout of shyness, the shop
owner reached in the jar himself and pulled out a handful,
placing the candies into the mom's bag. When they eventu-
ally got outside, the mom asked her son why he didn't get
the candies himself. The young boy smiled and promptly
replied, "His hand is bigger than mine."

God's blessings come bigger than anything we could ever piece together ourselves. He knows the desires of our hearts and what will truly cause us to be happy. Trusting Him to bless us in our marriage means letting go of our own attempts at fixing, creating, or manufacturing what we hope will become happiness. Rather, as with the young boy, it requires us to rest in the knowledge that God's hands and His heart are bigger than our own.

Let God surprise you with His blessings. Ask Him to delight you in your relationship. When you do, you will discover that God is far more romantic than you may have ever imagined. He loves to show up and show out, providing you with special reminders of His presence and His care. Look for them. They are there if you will take the time to ask and then believe.

Bear in mind that blessings don't always mean something like a new car or a new house. Blessings in your marriage may be an increased ability to appreciate and enjoy your spouse. Or it could be a heightened attraction toward each other. It might include an expansion of the impact you are making on those around you for good. And the awareness that as a couple you are able to do more for God when you work together as a team.

Never be too shy to ask God to bless you. Pray for this daily. In fact, pray the Scripture verse above daily. Then watch what God does both in you and through you as a married couple. Blessings abound when your hearts seek the Giver of all good things, and as you humble yourselves before Him in adoration, gratitude, and praise.

TRUSTING GOD
TO BLESS US
in our marriage
MEANS LETTING GO
OF OUR OWN ATTEMPTS
AT FIXING, CREATING,
OR MANUFACTURING
what we hope
WILL BECOME HAPPINESS.

Praising God

Heavenly Father, You are seated in the heavenlies—high and lifted up, above all of Your creation. Your Word tells us that every good and perfect gift comes from You, for You are the giver of all good things (James 1:17). You have already given us every spiritual blessing we are to have (Ephesians 1:3). It has already been determined by You to bless us. We only need to access this blessing through hearts set on You and align ourselves under You, asking You to pour out Your blessing onto us. Thank You for Your heart—a heart that takes joy in our own joy. Thank You for creating marriage so that we can experience the depth of true love and intimacy. Thank You that You embody romance in such a way that You provide ways for us to enjoy it with each other. Yours is a gracious heart, for which we are grateful.

Presenting the Situation

Use this portion to name areas in your life, circumstances, or in your marriage where you hope to have a greater portion of God's blessings. Get as specific as possible. If there are any situations that are currently causing you concern, be sure to name those as well. God's blessings have a way of wiping out worry and providing the atmosphere for gratitude to flow more freely. Be sure to thank God ahead of time for what you are asking Him to do. Thank Him with a spirit of expectation and hope, coupled with confidence in His ability and desire to answer. Make a note when you witness Him answering any of these specific prayers.

_____

_____

_____

_____

_____

Prayer for Blessing and Freedom

Gracious Lord, bless us indeed. Bless our home, bless our marriage, and bless our love for each other. Place Your hand upon us, and let Your hand be the funnel through which Your blessings flow. Lord, please expand the borders of our influence. Expand the areas in which we impact others for good. Expand our careers and our ability to move upward in them. Expand our hearts so that we better reflect Your own. Show us ways in which we can serve You and extend the blessings You have given to us. Keep us from evil that we might not experience pain. Keep us from being the cause of anyone else's pain, especially that of our spouse. Let us be a blessing in direct proportion to how You have blessed us, and let Your love shine through us, causing us to bless others through our smiles, a kind word, and as they witness the love which we have for each other in our marriage. In Christ's name, amen.

8

Sexual Intimacy

*May your fountain be blessed, and may you
rejoice in the wife of your youth. A loving doe, a
graceful deer—may her breasts satisfy you always,
may you ever be intoxicated with her love.*

PROVERBS 5:18-19

Preparing Our Hearts

One way to express intimacy in the Hebrew culture
came through the repetition of a name. We see this happen
multiple times in Scripture. Examples include:

- God calling out to Abraham as he is about to
  sacrifice Isaac (Abraham, Abraham—Genesis
  22:11)

- God sending Jacob on a journey of significance
  (Jacob, Jacob—Genesis 46:2)

- The message from the burning bush (Moses,
  Moses—Exodus 3:4)

- The whisper in the night to the prophet-in-
  training at the temple (Samuel, Samuel—
  1 Samuel 3:10)

- Jesus's comforting Martha in the midst of her brother's death (Martha, Martha—Luke 10:41)

- Jesus weeping over Jerusalem (O, Jerusalem, Jerusalem—Matthew 23:37)

The repetition of a name signifies a closeness and depth of care beyond the norm. Names reflect who we are. They are tied to us uniquely and personally. In fact, there are some cultures in Africa where a person's name is considered so intimate that it is only allowed to be spoken by an immediate relative. Everyone else in this region must use a form of father, mother, sister, or brother combined with another identifying factor when calling on that person.

Intimacy identifies a different level of relationship, whether it comes through language, proximity, or affection. Sexual intimacy offers us the deepest expression of closeness and care with another and, because of that, should be one of the most guarded and cherished aspects of the marriage relationship.

Guarding the marital sexual relationship does not only refer to protecting your heart and mind from external infringements or distractions. It also refers to finding new ways to protect your sexual relationship with your spouse from the futility of familiarity. This might include looking for new ways, locations, or times of day to fully enjoy each other. Sending loving text messages throughout the day or leaving notes around the house can also ignite emotions and feelings toward each other, setting the stage for sexual engagement later on. And while marital sex involves a depth beyond just the physical, being mindful that God has created the physical

THE MARITAL SEX LIFE
isn't something
THAT CHRISTIANS
ARE OFTEN
INSTRUCTED TO PRAY ABOUT;
however, it is
DESERVING OF PRAYER.

for each other's enjoyment can serve as an impetus for paying attention to personal appearance throughout the day and to wearing clothing that your spouse particularly likes. Cherishing your sexual relationship involves consistency, care, and discovery concerning what truly pleases each other.

When a couple both guards and cherishes the sexual intimacy in their marriage, they share a bond designed to give life, vitality, and enjoyment. In fact, God so wired the chemicals in our bodies that regular marital intercourse actually produces a chemical connection to each other. God has created different hormones to release before, during, and after sex in such a way that they enable married couples to strengthen the stability of their relationship through this shared gift.

Praising God

Heavenly Father, You created this gift of sexual intimacy, which is to be cherished, honored, and enjoyed within a marriage. You placed within us various hormones that give us the opportunity for great pleasure and a strengthening of our bond together. Thank You for creating sex and allowing us to have this to share together in our marriage. As we remain intimate with each other as a couple, we continue to experience a depth of love that reflects Your love for us. We praise and honor You for Your provision of delight, physical satisfaction, and intimacy.

Presenting the Situation

Use this portion to uncover areas in your sexual life which could use improvement and to write these down. It could be as simple as asking God to increase the level of attraction you feel for your spouse or that your spouse feels for you. Or it might be far more personal. Whatever it is you want God to work within, be sure to take it to Him in prayer. The marital sex life isn't something that Christians are often instructed to pray about; however, it is deserving of prayer. There is nothing off-limits with God when it comes to your prayer life. Share with Him how you feel, what you'd like to experience, and areas where you'd like Him to transform things. Then watch how He works in your life and in your spouse's life to bring about good.

_____

_____

_____

_____

_____

Prayer for Blessing and Freedom

Gracious Lord, thank You for giving us the opportunity to pray to You about our sex life. No one knows each of us better than You do. You know what we desire and how to achieve the fulfilling satisfaction of that desire. Teach us how to satisfy each other in ways that bring pleasure to us as well. Bless our sexual activity with creativity, fun, and an abiding connection. Keep spontaneity in our hearts and minds. And help us to remember the romance, soft touches, and gentle words that precede sex throughout our casual times together, or even when things get busy. I pray that our sex life will be so enjoyable that we will both look forward to it equally and with mutual enthusiasm. Heal any past or present wounds that may inhibit our full expression of sexual love. We thank You for this and so much more. In Christ's name, amen.

9

Influence

*Commit to the LORD whatever you do,
and he will establish your plans.*

PROVERBS 16:3

Preparing Our Hearts

Have you ever tried to stack dominoes in a line so that when you push the end, they all topple one by one? Most of us who have tried this have stopped at around 25 or 50 dominoes. It takes a lot of patience to carefully set up and measure each domino to ensure that the entire line falls in succession.

Can you imagine setting up 321,197 dominoes in that manner? That's exactly what Liu Yang of China did in 2011 to claim a spot in the *Guinness Book of World Records* for the most dominoes set up by an individual. As of the printing of this book, Liu still holds that record. But just as Rome wasn't built in a day, neither was Liu's record. In fact, it took him 38 days to get all of his dominoes in place. This attempt was part of a special New Year's Eve Celebration which had been scheduled to be broadcast on live TV. Not only did Liu work against his own self-prescribed pressures, but he also faced a deadline set in stone. With nearly all of China

NEVER SHRINK BACK

FROM WHAT MAY FEEL LIKE

simple acts of influence.

WHETHER IT'S SHARING A KIND WORD

IN A STRESSFUL MOMENT,

DOING A BIT MORE

AROUND THE HOUSE

THAN YOU NORMALLY DO,

OR GIVING A NECK MASSAGE

WHEN YOUR SPOUSE HAS HAD

A LONG DAY,

small impacts

BRING ABOUT NEW EXPERIENCES

AND FRESH JOY.

watching as Beijing TV aired this massive domino experience, Liu's 321,197 dominoes toppled one by one. Each one fell due to the impact of the one before it.

If only one domino failed to impact the domino after it, the entire experience would have been ruined. The existing Guinness record would not have been broken. And the New Year would have been rung in on a bit of a letdown for the viewers across the nation. Yet, because each domino successfully carried out its role of simply connecting with the domino nearest to it, the entire line of more than 300,000 fell successfully.

Sometimes we think of making an impact as something huge, such as going overseas to be a missionary, working in a soup kitchen every weekend, or adopting foster children. And while those acts of service are worthwhile and good, there is a lesson to learn from the dominoes. Each domino had only one thing to do—impact the domino beside it. When each domino did its part, the entire impact was made. Never shrink back from what may feel like simple acts of influence. Whether it's sharing a kind word in a stressful moment, doing a bit more around the house than you normally do, or giving a neck massage when your spouse has had a long day, small impacts bring about new experiences and fresh joy. And when they are compiled upon each other, they add up to something much larger altogether.

Liu's 300,000-plus dominoes fell because one domino fell at the very start. Scripture tells us in Zechariah 4:10, "Who dares despise the day of small things…" Small impacts usher in large waves when done consistently.

Praising God

Heavenly Father, You have created both of us to make an impact in the lives of those around us. We are to positively influence others toward You and Your love for them. You are our example of what that looks like. The many ways You have shown us kindness, mercy, and favor show us what it means to extend love to each other in our marriage and to those we know. Let our marriage relationship reflect Your heart so that when others see us as a couple, they recognize You in us. Even a small way of impacting others can create a wave of positivity flowing out from us. Just as the sun You set in the sky provides life through its energy, let Your energy be so evident and strong within us as a couple that others feel its warmth and increase their love for those around them. Thank You for giving us this opportunity to reflect Your love to a world in need of love.

Presenting the Situation

Use this portion to take some time and examine the impact you and your spouse are having on those around you. It may be the impact on your kids, extended family members, coworkers, church family, or neighbors. Whoever it is, identify areas where you could become more intentional about influencing others for good. Are there aspects of your marriage relationship where you could be a greater impact on each other, such as in the willingness to encourage more readily or support each other more consistently? It may involve a higher level of service to each other. Ask God to reveal ways in which you can be of greater impact throughout your daily life and in your marriage.

Prayer for Blessing and Freedom

Gracious Lord, give me wisdom and insight into my spouse's needs, personality, and desires. As I get to know my spouse on a more intimate level, I will be able to impact them more consistently. Help me to be an instrument of strength, positivity, and cheer to my spouse in every way possible. As we impact each other for good, we gain a greater ability to impact others as a couple. It starts with both of us doing small things for each other and doing them consistently. This creates a domino effect of good, trickling outward to those around us. Show us ways we can increase the joy in each other. Teach us how to cherish our marriage and, by cherishing it, to protect and preserve it. As we do these things, we will naturally increase the amount of good we seek to provide to each other, rather than merely looking for ways we can benefit from the relationship ourselves. Help us to always be outward focused in our thoughts, placing the needs and even the wants of our spouse above our own. In Christ's name, amen.

10

Mutual Service

Whatever you do, work at it with all your heart,
as working for the Lord, not for human masters.

Colossians 3:23

Preparing Our Hearts

A scene unfolded in the heart of the American Revolution where brave, worn, and weary men sought to repair a defensive barrier. This barrier was to protect civilians from any enemy attack. It took almost a week to repair this barrier as the men worked feverishly around the clock, knowing that the civilians were especially vulnerable without it.

On one particular day, a man in street clothes rode by on his horse and noticed another man shouting orders to the working soldiers but not helping them at all. The man in street clothes inquired why the supervisor wouldn't take the time to help seeing as this barrier was so critical. "Sir, I am a corporal!" the man responded to his question with an air of pride and assurance.

The man in street clothes simply smiled, dismounted from his own horse, and went to help the soldiers himself. At the end of the day as the soldiers made their way to their small bowl of dinner, the man in street clothes got back on

MAKE YOUR MARRIAGE
a relationship of
MUTUAL SERVICE,

AND YOU WILL DISCOVER

A LEVEL OF GRATITUDE

AND APPRECIATION

YOU MAY HAVE NEVER

known before.

THIS WILL PLEASE THE LORD.

his horse and rode up to the corporal. "Mr. Corporal," he said with a voice worn from the day's work, "next time you have a job like this and not enough men to do it—go to your commander-in-chief and let him know. And I will come help you again."

George Washington then rode off to his home, the corporal having learned a great lesson on leadership. No matter the position, role, or relationship we find ourselves in, the greatest act of love is one of service. Placing yourself higher than the person next to you falls within the realm of pride and entitlement, contrary to the spirit which God calls us to live out. We often forget in our marriage that serving our spouse is one of the most important things we can do. It doesn't need to be huge, but it does need to be consistent and carried out with authenticity. Whether it's running an errand, folding clothes, loading the dishwasher, washing a car, providing a drink, cooking a meal—whatever you do for your spouse, you are ultimately doing for the Lord. You are honoring God by honoring your husband or your wife.

You may also notice that the more you seek to serve your spouse, the more your spouse may seek to reciprocate the service. It's natural in all of us to want to return the good done to or for us. Make your marriage a relationship of mutual service, and you will discover a level of gratitude and appreciation you may have never known before. This will please the Lord and invite a greater depth of His love and blessing into your home.

Praising God

Heavenly Father, Jesus gave us an example of service as He knelt to wash the feet of His disciples. Knowing that one would betray Him, He still pressed on because serving others is done unto You to honor You and is not based on the warranting of it by another. Thank You for this model, but more than that, thank You for the even greater example of love when Christ went to the cross to die for our sins. We honor Your name and seek to reflect You in all that we do.

Presenting the Situation

Use this portion to focus on the area of service in your marriage. Are you willing to do acts of service for your spouse? Is your spouse willing to do them for you? Or is there a resistance to serving each other? Write down any areas where you or your spouse already serve each other with a right heart, and take time to thank God for these. Then, write down any areas where you hope to see an improvement. This might include wanting to see an improvement in an overall attitude toward serving, or it could include something as specific as drying the dishes. Remember to pray for God's hand of intervention in order to turn your marriage relationship into a place of mutual, intentional service.

_____

_____

_____

_____

_____

Prayer for Blessing and Freedom

Gracious Lord, let me start with myself. Work in my heart to notice ways I can better serve my spouse. I want to serve in a manner in which my spouse will feel my love. What are the areas where my spouse will really appreciate my serving them? Show me these, and nudge me when an opportunity comes up where I can serve. Give me a spirit of joy when it comes to serving my spouse, rather than a spirit of duty. And help me to remember that sexual intimacy—in those times when I may be tired or not in the mood for it—can also be seen as serving the needs or desires of my spouse. Let me release myself to my spouse fully and freely in all ways. Please also help my spouse to have an increased desire in their serving of me, while keeping me mindful to show appreciation when I am served. In Christ's name, amen.

11

Emotional Support

*Rejoice with those who rejoice; mourn
with those who mourn.*

ROMANS 12:15

Preparing Our Hearts

Few relationships give you as much opportunity to impact another person's life as a marriage relationship. It is within this context of close connection that you are positioned for your greatest potential to influence someone else. Now, that influence could be for good or could be for bad. It's up to you what kind of influence you offer your spouse. For example, when your spouse drives and makes a wrong turn—do you criticize or help? Do your words bring life into the situation, or do they bring negativity? You might feel this is a minor happening, but these moments build upon each other to establish the atmosphere of your relationship and home.

Another example involves how you speak about your spouse in public. Have you ever witnessed a couple where one spouse says something negative about the other in front of you? How did that make you feel? This type of talk instantly reveals a lack of respect and honor in the marriage.

It's true that marriage relationships will have disagreements or differences in opinion, but these things should be discussed privately. Public put-downs, even if done in a joking manner, leave a scar on the heart of the one who was put down. It is one of the fastest ways of cutting the emotional connection the two of you have together. This is because love, trust, and intimacy cannot thrive in a context of shame or embarrassment.

Thirdly, how do you respond to your spouse when he or she shares dreams or hopes they would like to someday live out? Even if these dreams or hopes seem outlandish to you, providing the space for your spouse to dream deepens the level of attachment between you. It is up to God to open or close doors for your spouse. You don't need to be the one to douse dreams which you feel may be a bit too lofty. Let encouragement be a way of life in your marriage, and you will begin to develop a connection that goes beyond the "everyday-ness" of life. Far too often, men or women lean on coworkers or friends for the encouragement they need. Yet, the marriage relationship ought to be the greatest source of emotional support, whether dealing with loss or disappointment or sharing a vision for the future. Nurture this aspect of your marriage and, in so doing, you will nurture a friendship and camaraderie which will cause your relationship to be deeply satisfying and emotionally stimulating.

Praising God

Heavenly Father, thank You for allowing me to dream. I praise You that You have made me in Your image and placed creativity and hopes in my heart. Life is a journey with opportunities and loss, but You make

PROVIDING

THE SPACE FOR

your spouse to dream

DEEPENS THE LEVEL

OF ATTACHMENT

between you.

this journey possible through Your steadfast love and support. You are always near when I need a shoulder to lean on. You provide strength through Your Word. Your love gives me the power to believe when life's disappointments could cause me to doubt. I honor and worship You for who You are and what You allow me to pursue. Thank You for establishing marriage as that place where we both can find friendship, love, and encouragement. Life comes with so many challenges and difficulties. It can be enough to dampen any spirit. But You have given us each other in our marriage in order to be a buffer from the darkness and a light to bring in hope.

Presenting the Situation

Use this portion to think through the tone of your words and responses to your spouse. Are they filtered through a lens of negativity, or are they punctuated by positive, life-giving thoughts? You hold a tremendous amount of power with regard to your spouse and their overall mood, vision, and decisions. This power is located in your mouth. Ask God to make you more aware of what you say to your spouse. Spend a few days keeping a journal to write down anything you say that is negative. You and your spouse are a team. When you negatively impact your spouse, you are negatively impacting yourself by default. Let your words and your actions reflect hope and belief, instilling trust in your relationship.

Prayer for Blessing and Freedom

Gracious Lord, help us to encourage each other, rather than try to correct each other. Give us hearts that see the good rather than the risks. As we trust You more fully, we can trust each other more freely. You are ultimately in control, and You have called us to love each other in both word and deed. Let honor be sprinkled into everything we say, especially publicly. Let others notice our interactions with each other and desire the same level of honor and trust in their own marriage. Let us be a model of mutual love and respect to everyone who comes into contact with us. And let us feel cherished by each other through how we encourage and emotionally support each other in every moment of every day. In Christ's name, amen.

12

Attraction

*May the wine go straight to my beloved,
flowing gently over lips and teeth. I belong
to my beloved, and his desire is for me.*

Song of Songs 7:9-10

Preparing Our Hearts

Most of us took the time to try to look as nice as we could when we were dating, or to try and maintain an open, positive spirit. We spent the extra effort to pick out what clothes we were wearing and to make sure our hair was in place. We limited our complaints or outward displays of disappointment and frustration. Many of us even tried to watch our weight during that season. We knew the importance of attraction in a dating relationship and sought to do our part in looking attractive to our dating partner as well as being attractive in our attitudes and actions.

Yet, somewhere along the line, many of us lost this attentiveness to our own attractiveness after marriage. It could be the futility of the familiar or the duties that drained our energy which contributed to this loss of effort. Whatever the case, attraction within a marriage is just as important to pay attention to, if not more so, than in a dating relationship. Why? Because the habitual has a way of dulling the shine or lessening the mystique. Unfortunately, the tyranny of the typical may lower appeal rather than increase it.

Saying "I do" didn't reduce any hormones or harden any hearts. We are human and, whether married or not, most of us still enjoy the feeling of attraction. Which is why maintaining your personal appearance, hygiene, and attitudes while married ought to be a high value for both spouses.

What are some things you can do to remain attractive to your spouse? You can start by revisiting the things you did when you were dating. Attractiveness is unique to each person. It doesn't mean dressing up for everyone or being pencil thin—or even wearing makeup if you are a woman. But whatever it was that you did when dating which caused your spouse to be drawn to you, consider whether or not you are still doing these things now.

It may have been your vitality, laugh, or free spirit that caused your spouse to be attracted to you when dating, more so than your looks. If you don't know what it was, then simply ask. For some people, attraction is related to the mind, conversation, or vivacity. For others, it's a spirit, or the way you walk, or your frequency of touch. Take time to talk about this as a couple, and focus on the things that bring about a greater attraction to each other. But be sure to do so with a heart of encouragement, not criticism.

Attraction will often increase in marriage as you and your spouse deepen your level of intimacy and enhance your shared experiences. What evokes attraction can also change over time. Be sure to revisit this topic every so often as a couple so that each of you can identify what makes you more

ATTRACTION WITHIN

a marriage

IS JUST AS IMPORTANT

TO PAY ATTENTION TO,

IF NOT MORE SO,

THAN IN A

dating relationship.

attractive to your spouse, and focus on how to embody that for them. Remember, you are a gift to your spouse—a gift to delight in, honor, and enjoy. As they are also to you. Have fun with it. Flirt. Send loving texts. Wear that shirt they love. Maintain that gaze longer than necessary. Wink. Share one side of a booth when eating out. Keep your attraction to each other alive, and you will find that communication as well as mutual decision-making will come more naturally to you as well.

Praising God

Heavenly Father, You crafted our world with such beauty. You paid attention to all the minute details that surround us—from flowers to trees to mountains to birds to snowflakes to the way our bodies were made. You have gifted each of us with so much beauty and life. It inspires us and nourishes our soul with strength. I praise You for Your creativity and design. You lift my spirit with Your creations, and You have given me the opportunity to lift the spirit of my spouse through my own life as well. Thank You for this ability. I do not take it for granted.

Presenting the Situation

Use this portion to honestly assess how much importance you assign to looking or being attractive for your spouse. Since you can only control what you do, be sure to focus on yourself in this section. Are there things that you have let slide—whether it's controlling your moods, what you say, or what you wear, to name a few? Is there anything you could do in order to increase your spouse's attraction to you? Write down some things you can work on. Then pray and ask God for wisdom and self-discipline to improve in those areas.

Prayer for Blessing and Freedom

Gracious Lord, give me insight into how I can increase my attractiveness to my spouse. Help me to choose my words wisely so what I say is sweet and affirming, rather than complaining or demanding. Give me energy so that I can bless my spouse with vitality, enthusiasm, and joy. Remind me to stay aware of how I look and what I wear. And let me be a source of pleasure to my spouse mentally, emotionally, and physically. In the same way, help my spouse to be attentive to what makes them attractive to me. Reignite the flame of passion and romance between us, and keep it lit. In Christ's name, amen.

13

Attentiveness

*And over all these virtues put on love, which
binds them all together in perfect unity.*

<small>COLOSSIANS 3:14</small>

Preparing Our Hearts

The technology company Microsoft conducted a large-scale study on thousands of people a few years ago in Canada to measure attention spans. They sought to compare the results to ones prior to the onset of digital media and smartphones. What their research turned up was alarming. Not only had attention spans nearly halved since the increase of social media and the like, but they now measured less than that of a goldfish. Yes, according to scientific data, a goldfish could hold a thought longer than the average human being.

While our dearth in attention spans can have negative impacts on our work or even on our hobbies, one of the more critical areas it can impact is our marriages. Relational attentiveness is a key component to nurturing valuable assets such as trust, understanding, empathy, and more. Yet, when spouses can barely carry on a conversation without having to check in on social media midway through, or can't sit through a meal without their phone nearby to

BE INTENTIONAL ABOUT
your times together.
PUT YOUR PHONES AWAY
DURING MEALS OR DISCUSSIONS.
MAKE EYE CONTACT,
and try to keep it
THROUGHOUT THE CONVERSATION.
RECOGNIZE NONVERBAL CUES
THAT CAN GIVE YOU A GLIMPSE
INTO YOUR SPOUSE'S NEEDS,
WANTS, OR MOODS.

access at will, growing these essential areas of relational connection becomes challenging.

Just as the Scripture verse chosen for this subject outlines how love binds all virtues together in perfect unity, attentiveness binds two people together relationally. Consider how you feel when you share something that means a lot to you or something you did that day with your spouse, only to discover they didn't hear you at all. They may have been present, but their mind had gone on its own journey elsewhere. This lack of attentiveness creates gaps in the grooves that connect us, causing us to drift apart rather than draw closer together. The enthusiasm with which you first shared what you were saying is rarely matched once you have been asked to repeat it. In fact, oftentimes you may simply say, "Never mind."

Lack of attentiveness can have a devastating impact on any relationship. Setting it outside of the context of marriage may help bring this to light. In a work environment, if your boss were to give you information or instructions on a task they were needing you to complete, you would most certainly pay attention. You might even take notes. Why? Because your boss's view of you depends on how well you perform the request. Far too many of us will pay greater attention at work than we ever do to our spouse. It's not because we don't realize the value of attentiveness. Rather, it's often because we become lazy. Laziness can be an outgrowth of taking your spouse for granted. When you take your spouse for granted, you can become negligent in how much you engage emotionally and mentally with them. This negligence or dismissiveness can contribute to the breakdown of the relational enjoyment.

In order to overcome inattentiveness in your marriage, be intentional about your times together. Put your phones away during meals or discussions. Make eye contact, and try to keep it throughout the conversation. Recognize non-verbal cues that can give you a glimpse into your spouse's needs, wants, or moods. Seek to connect by placing your hand on their arm when talking. Sometimes a simple touch can draw someone's attention to what you are saying. Rather than watching television or movies all the time, pick out books to read together. Read to each other. This exercises your mind muscles so that your attention spans will increase when needed most. Most importantly, cultivate the art of listening. That may mean slowing down from the hectic pace of life in order to listen. Attentiveness in your marriage will enable you to better know, understand, and support each other in every area of life.

Praising God

Heavenly Father, You listen when I pray. You hear me when I call. You respond when I ask. You are there when I seek You. You are not a distant God whose attention I can never grab. You are not an insecure Being who looks for significance in appearing to be busy. You are good, gracious, and willing to listen. I praise You for the value You show me by hearing my heart. I honor You for the kindness You extend by responding to my smallest of requests. I smile because I know that You smile when I remember to say thank You for all You do. That's how much You care. You are the model of attentiveness, and I thank You for that.

Presenting the Situation

Use this portion to consider how many interruptions you allow into your time with your spouse. While every moment can't be dedicated to paying complete attention to each other, are there times and opportunities where you could both be more attentive? Life has demands, and interruptions do occur, but how many of these are necessary at the moment? These are the questions you can ask yourself and discuss together. Finding ways to put your phones away while you talk or walk together can provide a greater opportunity for attentiveness. Or turning off the television or movies may encourage you to fill the space with your own thoughts. Nurture your connection through intentional attentiveness whether in the car, at meals, or simply when you are together.

_____

_____

_____

_____

_____

Prayer for Blessing and Freedom

Gracious Lord, remind me to remain attentive to my spouse and family members. It's so easy to get sucked into social media or other things that seek my attention. But, Lord, I want to show my spouse how much I value them, and one way to do this is by giving them my full attention when we are together or talking. Help my spouse to understand my need for their attentiveness to me as well. Convict us in this area in order to prompt us toward a more consistent level of communication and understanding. Give us patience with each other, and help us develop a genuine interest in what the other is thinking, feeling, or doing. And when other family members' needs interrupt our attentiveness toward each other as a couple, help us to quickly return after taking care of what needed to be done. Thank You for bringing this important subject to our attention. In Christ's name, amen.

14

Faultfinding

A person's wisdom yields patience; it is to
one's glory to overlook an offense.

PROVERBS 19:11

Preparing Our Hearts

An elderly grandmother went to lunch with her grand-daughter, who was about to get married. The granddaughter had always admired her grandparents' marriage. She wanted to remain married for over 50 years just like they did. Thus, she took this opportunity to glean some wisdom from her grandma about how to keep a marriage strong.

"Grandma," she asked, "what did you do in order to have such a long and satisfying marriage?"

"Oh, it's simple," her grandma replied without hesitation. "When I got married, I decided to list ten of your granddad's faults which, for the sake of our marriage, I would choose to overlook."

"You did?" the soon-to-be bride asked. "What are some of them?" she continued, looking for an example to help her choose her own.

"I don't know," her grandma responded. "I actually never did list them. But whenever Granddad did something

GOD INSTRUCTS US

how to maintain

A SPIRIT OF LOVE AND UNITY

IN OUR MARRIAGE

WHEN HE TELLS US

IN PROVERBS

THAT IT IS TO OUR OWN GLORY

to overlook

ANOTHER'S FAULTS.

that made me fume, I'd just say to myself, 'Lucky for him that's one of the ten.'"

If you are married, you know by now that you did not marry a perfect human being. Everyone has faults, weaknesses, and even oddities. Oftentimes, these don't come to the surface until after you say "I do." But living with someone 24/7 reveals a lot. Unfortunately, faultfinding is one of the most tragic things to happen to a marriage. Primarily because there are plenty of faults to be found on both sides.

But God instructs us how to maintain a spirit of love and unity in our marriage when He tells us in Proverbs that it is to our own glory to overlook another's faults. One way to do this is to always start by giving the benefit of the doubt. Rather than jump to conclusions or rash judgments about your spouse's faults, mistakes, or peculiarities, assume the best first. Let that be the foundation for your questions as you seek to understand the situation at hand. Then, if there truly is a fault in play (which there will be from time to time), overlook it. Let it pass. Let it go. Not because we are saying so, but because God is.

Rather than focusing on the faults of your spouse, focus on what he or she does well. Let your words reflect an awareness of their strengths, gifts, and contributions to your relationship and home. You'll be amazed at how your spouse will seek to do even more positive things in your presence when you point out the good and not the bad. Affirmation goes a long way toward creating an atmosphere of acceptance and mutual affection.

And if giving the benefit of the doubt isn't the way you naturally roll, you may want to consider how many faults you've brought to the table as well. Showing grace to each other in your marriage relationship rests on the foundational truth that marriage is comprised of two imperfect people seeking to live in harmony and grace. Faults abound, yes. In everyone. But they do not need to dominate your thoughts or conversations or influence your actions. If the fault is at a level that needs to be addressed for the sake of the relationship, address it. But express your disappointments in a spirit that shows honor. Be mindful not to criticize the person while bringing light to a behavior that brought you pain or concern. Then, once shared, seek a solution or approach toward improvement together. Once decided, move on.

While the following verses refer only to women, the principles in them transcend gender and can apply to both husbands and wives. They reveal to us the destructive nature of faultfinding to any marriage:

- Better to live on a corner of the roof than share a house with a quarrelsome wife (Proverbs 25:24).

- A quarrelsome wife is like the dripping of a leaky roof in a rainstorm (Proverbs 27:15).

An atmosphere of faultfinding will destroy the intimacy in any marriage, whether it comes from the wife or the husband—or both. If this is something you've experienced in your marriage or do yourself, it is best to seek its removal entirely and look for ways to build each other up through what you think, say, and do.

Praising God

Heavenly Father, You say that it is to my glory to

overlook a fault. Also, that patience is a virtue and grace a gift. These are things that You have already shown time and time again. If You held my sins and faults against me, I would have no hope. Instead, You willingly forgive and even provide the pathway for that forgiveness to take place through the sacrifice of Jesus Christ. Receive my praise for Your patience. Accept my worship for Your willingness to forgive. I honor Your heart which so readily overlooks my faults. Mold me into Your likeness in my character and emotions, Lord, so that I can reflect You in my marriage.

Presenting the Situation

Use this portion to identify patterns of criticizing or fault-finding that may have crept into your marriage relationship. It could be in yourself, in your spouse, or even in both of you. (If your marriage doesn't struggle in this area, then use this space to thank God and ask Him to continue to protect your marriage from this happening.) Once your patterns are identified, pray through each area and ask God for wisdom and awareness on how to overcome them. Seek to replace anything negative that would normally come from your mouth with something positive. Choose something affirming rather than derogatory. As you continue to do these things, a tendency toward finding fault will lessen. If it is your spouse who is quick to find fault with you, ask God to intervene in their life and convict them of this sin. Then pray faithfully that the Lord will transform your spouse's mind, heart, and words by the power of His Spirit into that which brings life into your marriage instead.

Prayer for Blessing and Freedom

Gracious Lord, help me to be quick to hear, slow to speak, and slow to anger. Help me to be mindful of what I say both to and about my spouse. Rather than look to correct my spouse, I ask that You help me seek to encourage my spouse. Create in me a clean heart and a pure spirit which seeks to bring good and not bad to those around me. Please cause my spouse not to fall into the trap of faultfinding regarding me either. Give my spouse self-control over what they say to me and about me. Enable my spouse to recognize the good in me and overlook my faults. Thank You for giving us both the ability to improve in this area of our marriage as we trust in You to do just that. In Christ's name, amen.

15

Transitional Stress

*You will go out in joy and be led forth in peace; the
mountains and hills will burst into song before you,
and all the trees of the field will clap their hands.*

Isaiah 55:12

Preparing Our Hearts

Life comes with transition. Whether it's a new job, new
house, new child or grandchild, and even something as
small as a new hairstyle, we face change throughout our
lives. Some of us are more adept at change. Others of us
resist it. Some of us can adapt quickly. Others are slow
to process change. Some change brings positivity. Other
change causes loss. If we were honest, even age changes us.
There's nothing we can do to avoid this inevitable aspect
of life.

One thing that will never change about life and marriage is that there will always be change.

Understanding how to approach change emotionally,
spiritually, and mentally can allow transition to transform
our marriage into something stronger and more viable than
ever before. Contrary to popular belief, stress doesn't have to
be a negative thing. How you and your spouse view stress,

as well as how you choose to respond to it, has everything to do with whether it leaves a positive or undesirable imprint on your home. God has gifted us with the ability to decide how we react to life's transitions.

Did you know that the muscles in your body become stronger during rest, not during a workout and its stress? What the stress on your muscles does is break down the muscle protein that exists in your body structure. But the actual development of stronger muscles takes place as your body rests. When your body has the opportunity to repair and replace the damaged muscle fibers by fusing muscle fibers together to create new myofibrils, it builds tougher, more resilient muscles. A bodybuilder who doesn't take the time to respond to their workout through adequate rest will actually slow down the process of developing strength and endurance through greater muscle mass.

Likewise, how we respond to transitions and, even more importantly, how we allow our spouse to respond to transition will determine whether the stress of the transitions will strengthen us or, rather, weaken us over time. We must be willing to view the stress of transition as a developmental process and necessary part of life. We also must be willing to provide the space necessary for what stress may produce in ourselves and each other—times of lessened energy, distracted focus, or roller-coaster emotions. Placing unrealistic expectations or demands on ourselves or each other to keep our affection or even our mood consistently heightened during times of transition may only lead to disappointment. Give time for the transition while seeking to solidify

UNDERSTANDING
how to approach change
EMOTIONALLY, SPIRITUALLY,

AND MENTALLY

CAN ALLOW TRANSITION

TO TRANSFORM OUR MARRIAGE

into something

STRONGER AND MORE VIABLE

THAN EVER BEFORE.

and focus on core values such as mutual respect, kindness, patience, and service.

Other strategies for strengthening your marriage through the inevitability of transition include intentionally lightening the mood or atmosphere, whether through fun music, humor, witty banter, or simply letting each other's more tired emotions roll off your back. Don't take every response personally. Give the other person the benefit of the doubt. Show grace. Understand that they are experiencing change, and their nonverbal cues or even their tone may simply reflect their momentary stress and not be directed at or caused by you. In short, just as you would recognize a weight lifter's inability to carry on an in-depth conversation with you due to the current needs of the workout, be aware that transitional stress depletes emotional and physical energy as well. Adjust your expectations of and demands on each other to that reality.

Another strategy includes verbalizing or even internalizing the positives. Rather than focusing on the loss, change, or adjustments, look for ways to emphasize your highest values, whether they be each other, family, the things that have gone well, or the hope of the future. Continuing to speak about negative emotions or events will only reinforce them. What you speak transforms what you think. More so, what you say to each other—and how you say it—will affect how the transitional stress either grows weaker or damages your relationship. "A gentle answer turns away wrath, but a harsh word stirs up anger" (Proverbs 15:1).

Lastly, encourage each other in the Lord. Philippians 4:13 tells us, "I can do everything through Christ, who gives me strength" (NLT). Remind yourself of this. Remind your spouse of this. Rehearse it in your thoughts and words if need be, knowing that the result on the other side of the change you currently face is intended by God to bring you both good in your relationship, and not harm (Jeremiah 29:11; Romans 8:28). When you decide to embrace the transitional stress rather than fight it, being open to change—letting go of what is in the past and anticipating the new—you will, like an athlete committed to strength training, enjoy the results the right response to stress can produce.

Praising God

Heavenly Father, You are a God who changes not. Despite the transitions around me, You are the One who remains constant. You are ever present and always reliable. Thank You for Your consistency in a life that fluctuates often like the wind. I praise You for the ability You have given to me and to us in our marriage to rely on You. Your character is solid. Your Word true. Your presence steadfast and never lost. Thank You that You offer this to us like a lighthouse in a storm of stress, a beacon in the battling gusts of life's many unknowns.

Presenting the Situation

Use this portion to acknowledge any transitional stress which may have become a part of your marriage or home. It could be work change, a change in your financial situation, a move, or a change in family dynamics such as a new baby or graduation of a child. Whatever the change or changes may be, your awareness of them and how they impact your emotional, spiritual, and physical capacity and makeup will help to reduce any negative impact they bring into your marriage. Write out any specific transitions or failures to respond positively to transitions that you would like to see the Lord intervene in and work out for good.

_____

_____

_____

_____

_____

Prayer for Blessing and Freedom

Gracious Lord, help our marriage relationship to grow deeper and stronger as a result of any transitional stress we experience. Give us a greater respect for each other from the process of going through changes together. Show us how to accommodate each other's lower energy levels, rather than to feel neglected or rejected by them. Teach us how to truly encourage through words, patience, a gentle touch, gifts, or whatever it may be. Open our hearts and our eyes toward each other's needs during this season so that we can be more mindful to seek to meet them. And help us also to show ourselves grace by allowing rest when we need it too. Let us not lose any humor, joy, or mutual attraction, but rather increase it as we pursue the positive results of transitional stress together through knowing that Your intended outcome is for our good. In Christ's name, amen.

16

Communication

To answer before listening—that is folly and shame.

PROVERBS 18:13

Preparing Our Hearts

Communication can make or break a relationship. When it's carried out well, it allows the relationship to grow, develop, and deepen. When it's done poorly, even minor misunderstandings can evolve into mountains of conflict. Or, worse yet, when marital communication doesn't take place much at all, it reduces the engagement of the couple to that of mere strangers. Married couples who live in a communication-less home often feel as if they are living alone and have no one with whom to share their life. It can also lead to a sense that each spouse has to carry the full weight of life's troubles and trials on their own.

A funny illustration on miscommunication can bring the need for accurate communication in a marriage to light. Many years ago—before the onset of the Internet—there was a woman who had been raised in a strict, proper environment her entire life. Her speech was always delicate and elegant. She simply didn't say nor write words that could be construed as distasteful. Thus, when she had planned a trip to Florida, she carefully handwrote a letter to the campground she had hoped to stay at on her trip. She wanted to make her reservations but also to determine how many toilets they had, and how close to the campground areas they were. Yet, this prim and proper woman could not bring herself to write the word *toilet*, so she just used a more old-fashioned term: *bathroom commode.*

However, as she went to pen the words *bathroom commode,* embarrassment flooded her once again, and she gave in to simply using the initials *BC.* She wrote, "Does the campground have its own BC, and if so, how far away is it?"

The campground manager hadn't been raised in a strict nor proper environment at all. He had no idea what *BC* was referring to. So, he set about to find out from his staff at the campground. As each person sought to determine what the woman could be inquiring about, someone finally came up with the idea that she was asking if there was a local Baptist church. Surely, it must be insiders talk for Christians, they thought.

Assuming this, the campground manager drafted the following response:

Dear Madam:

I am thrilled to inform you that the BC is only five miles to the north of the campground. It has the capacity to seat 250 people at one time. While I acknowledge that may seem like quite a distance if you are in the state of going regularly, you will be delighted to discover that most people actually bring their lunches with them and make a day of it.

The last time I took my own wife was six weeks ago. Unfortunately, it was so crowded that we had to stand the entire time. But since then, they added more seats so you should be able to locate a seat if you arrive early enough.

If you prefer, I will go with you on your first visit so I can introduce you to some people. I'd be more than happy to do that!

Yours sincerely,
The Campground Manager

Misunderstandings and miscommunication can lead to a world of difference in the results we had hoped to obtain. Oftentimes, this happens in a marriage when one spouse chooses to speak before actively listening. There are many things that contribute to this, but none of which are good or helpful. Effective communication requires attention. It requires listening first. It even requires being aware of your spouse's nonverbal communication. The majority of all communication comes through nonverbal means. When marital communication is limited to text messages or quick sharing in passing as life goes on all around you, couples will neglect to truly hear and understand what the other is needing to say. This can lead to feelings of isolation, increases in conflict, and general misunderstandings.

To nurture your marital communication, set aside specific time simply for communication. Place digital media aside, and give your spouse your complete attention. Make this a regular, daily occurrence. And practice the art of hearing and repeating in your own words the overall summary of what was said in order to be sure you are both on the same page before moving forward.

Praising God

Heavenly Father, You have given us the gift of communication in so many ways. It comes across in our tone of voice, our posture, our facial expressions, and our words. You have made us in Your image so that we can communicate in more ways than just one. I praise You because of Your various ways of communicating with us, whether it's through Your presence, peace, or the expression of Your creativity through Your creation. I honor You for the ways You make Yourself known to us. You speak through Your Word, but Your Holy Spirit also translates and applies spiritual principles to our hearts. You impress upon us certain things at specific times to nudge us in the right direction. You are always communicating. If we will simply listen, we will hear. As Jesus often said, "Whoever has ears, let them hear…" Hearing is intentional. Thank You for giving us the ability to hear when we apply ourselves.

Presenting the Situation

Use this portion to outline the strengths you see in your marriage relationship regarding communication. List as many examples as possible. Perhaps one or both of you are good at listening. Or maybe you already carve out time for intentional communication with each other. Be sure to spend time thanking God for the communication skills He's developed in you already. Then, spend some time praying for wisdom on how to improve in the areas where communication

Effective communication
REQUIRES ATTENTION.
IT REQUIRES LISTENING FIRST.
IT EVEN REQUIRES
being aware
OF YOUR SPOUSE'S
NONVERBAL COMMUNICATION.

may be weak or lacking. Ask God for insight into how to develop these areas more fully. Write out specific things you can do to try and communicate more effectively as a couple.

_____

_____

_____

_____

_____

Prayer for Blessing and Freedom

Gracious Lord, let our words always be seasoned with grace as we speak to each other in our marriage. Help us to refrain from negativity or life-stealing tones and words. When there is disappointment, let it be expressed with honor and respect. When there is frustration, let it be punctuated with grace. When we experience boredom or irritation, let our words and nonverbal communication give encouragement in order to turn the tide and uplift the atmosphere. Help us both to be intentional in how we communicate with each other so that we use this gift as an instrument for nurturing our home and hearts. And in all things, enable us to know how to speak clearly when expressing our emotions and/or needs to each other. In Christ's name, amen.

17

Conflict

*The end of a matter is better than its
beginning, and patience is better than pride.
Do not be quickly provoked in your spirit,
for anger resides in the lap of fools.*

ECCLESIASTES 7:8-9

Preparing Our Hearts

The story is told about a married couple who had been together for over 50 years. For all intents and purposes, it appeared that they had handled their conflict well throughout their lengthy marriage. It was only when the wife grew so ill that she had to be hospitalized that the husband discovered the secret to their ease of reconciling conflict. This secret came stored in a box.

On the top shelf of their shared closet sat a box that the wife had requested that the husband never open. It was only when she was ill and hospitalized that he asked if he could open it. She agreed. Inside the box, he found two crocheted dolls and $75,000 in cash. The husband inquired about the contents, and the wife promptly replied, "When we got married, my mom gave me advice that whenever we faced

RATHER THAN

allowing conflict

TO CREATE A DIVISION

IN YOUR RELATIONSHIP,

WHEN YOU CHOOSE

to approach it

WITH WISDOM,

IT CAN ACTUALLY PRODUCE

SOMETHING GOOD.

conflict, I was to simply let it go and place my focus elsewhere on crocheting a doll."

The husband beamed with pride. The box held only two dolls. He felt like the hero of all husbands! "But what about the money?" he asked her, not sure where that had come from.

"Oh, that?" she responded. "Well, I've sold the dolls for $5 each over the years."

This humorous tale gives insight into how much conflict can occur in a marriage. Conflict arises on the small and the large things in life. It could be something as simple as where or what to eat for dinner. It can, as you probably already know, involve things of much more deep concern as well. Yet, rather than allowing conflict to create a division in your relationship, when you choose to approach it with wisdom, it can actually produce something good. Dennis Rainey, the president of Family Life Ministries, offers these six steps for resolving conflict in a marriage:

1. Resolving conflict requires knowing, accepting, and adjusting to your differences.

2. Resolving conflict requires defeating selfishness.

3. Resolving conflict requires pursuing the other person.

4. Resolving conflict requires loving confrontation.

5. Resolving conflict requires forgiveness.

6. Resolving conflict requires returning a blessing for an insult.[1]

---

[1] Rainey, Dennis, "6 Steps for Resolving Conflict in Marriage," https://www.familylife.com/articles/topics/marriage/staying-married/resolving-conflict/6-steps-for-resolving-conflict-in-marriage, accessed 7/25/18.

Just as important as resolving conflict may be, how you go about resolving it can make quite the impact on your marriage. Remember to always maintain a level of class and dignity in your speech, nonverbal communication, and the timing of when you choose to address conflict. Treating each other with dignity will do wonders for not only the atmosphere of your home but also the love in your relationship. A marriage, of all places, should be highlighted with hearts of honor. When you keep honor and dignity as the standard, you'll discover that working through conflict becomes a natural outcome of your everyday life. You'll also see it overflow into your other relationships at work or in your extended family.

Praising God

Heavenly Father, You chose to address the conflict that my sin brought between us by humbling Yourself through Christ Jesus and His death on the cross. You took the upper road. You swallowed Your pride. You lowered Yourself to provide the pathway for our relational restoration with You. I honor You for how You have honored us. I worship You for how You have esteemed us as Your children. I worship You for the ways in which You have granted each of us dignity. May Your model of meekness serve as our guide in our marriage.

Presenting the Situation

Use this portion to talk to the Lord about any ways conflict has presented unhealthy patterns of relating to each other in your marriage. Ask God to help you identify any of these destructive patterns of speech, avoidance, codependence, or aggressiveness. Then seek the Spirit's guidance on how to improve upon these weaknesses and strengthen your ability to resolve conflict with class and dignity. Also consider positive examples of where you already succeed in this area as a couple, and spend time thanking the Lord for these.

Prayer for Blessing and Freedom

Gracious Lord, make us instruments of peace toward each other in our marriage. Where there is division, give us the ability to seek unity. Sow grace in our spirits. Grow acceptance in our hearts. Instill honor in our minds. Let our relationship reflect Your own image. Make us an inspiration to couples around us as a way to handle conflict with class. Even in times when we are not experiencing conflict, give us an openness with each other that will facilitate increased communication. Let conflict strengthen us as a couple as it provides insight into each other and opportunities for compassion to be showcased. In Christ's name, amen.

18

Finances

For where your treasure is, there
your heart will be also.

MATTHEW 6:21

Preparing Our Hearts

There once was a man who lived like a miser. He worked diligently all of his life in order to save up his money. His wife had strict allowances on what she could or could not spend. By the time he approached his death, he had set aside a small fortune by most people's standards. His wife thought she just might get to spend some of it upon his passing. But, no, the husband requested that she put all of his money in his casket with him when he was buried.

Being the dutiful wife she had always been, she agreed to do just that.

When the funeral was about to come to a close, she walked up to the casket and placed a small envelope just under his hand. She kissed his forehead and said, "There you go, my love." The pastor standing nearby had been made aware of her promise but wondered as to the wisdom of letting so much money get buried in a casket. He turned to her and whispered as she began to walk away,

WHEN COUPLES

recognize it is not

"YOUR MONEY"

OR "MY MONEY"

BUT RATHER "OUR MONEY,"

THEY WILL BE ON THEIR WAY

TO FINANCIAL FREEDOM

as well as

THE FREEDOM IN THEIR

RELATIONSHIP TO FOCUS

ON THINGS

BEYOND FINANCES.

encouraging her to reconsider her decision. But rather than relent, the dutiful wife simply said, "Pastor, I cannot go back on my promise to my husband."

Then, as she proceeded to walk away, she turned to the pastor, smiled, and said, "I wrote him a check."

Ah, money and marriage. You may not be surprised to hear that regular fights about finances is one of the top predictors of whether or not a marriage will end up in divorce. A recent study by TD Bank found that over 60 percent of all couples felt that the other spouse overspent. Money and marriage can be a source of strain for couples, whether they earn a lot or a little by the world's standards. Decisions on what to spend and when can literally suck the air of affection right out the windows of any home.

What's more, hardly any married couples earn a similar or equal income. Due to various differences such as stages in life, degrees, or tenure of employment, spouses will often find a disparity between what one or the other earns. If one or both spouses feel that they can leverage their income over the other because they earn more or feel that their work is more challenging, arguments will be underwritten by resentment regarding spending. It isn't until couples recognize the reality that as a couple it is not "your money" or "my money" but rather "our money" that they will be on their way to financial freedom as well as the freedom in their relationship to focus on things beyond finances.

Matthew 6:21 tells us plainly that where our treasure is, there our heart will be also. If you or your spouse place a higher value on money and spending choices than on each other, then you have set money as an idol in your own home.

You have made it a treasure that will eclipse your own heart. A heart cannot be set on two things equally. Understanding the value you (or your spouse) place on money or financial decisions can help you know whether that is something you need to address in your marriage. Other things you can do to alleviate disagreements on financial matters include possibly setting up individual bank accounts for individual spending, as well as one joint account. Discussing what percentage of each person's paycheck goes into the joint account toward joint bills can give a sense of equity in responsibility. Also setting up times for financial planning conversations where you talk about goals and steps to take to meet those goals will help in alleviating confusion about money between the two of you. This will come as no surprise, but choosing to live debt free will also significantly reduce the amount of felt financial pressure upon your marriage. These steps and more give healthy boundaries for approaching what can be a volatile area of a marriage so it can be transformed into an area of shared understanding, growth, and enjoyment.

Praising God

Heavenly Father, You own the cattle on a thousand hills, and You are our Source. Everything else is just a resource. All good things, including our finances, originate from You. By focusing more on money than on Your precepts and principles for our marriage, we set money as a higher power than You. We give money more honor than we give to You. Essentially, we seek to praise money rather than You. Forgive us, Lord, for the times when we have worried, argued, or fought over finances in our marriage. Have mercy on us, God, and align our thoughts underneath the truth that You are the Source of all money. Any issue we have with money should be taken to You and presented to You with a heart of thanksgiving. This is how You've instructed us to handle worries in Your Word. Thank You for providing for us in so many ways. Thank You for being our Source in every way.

Presenting the Situation

Use this portion to let your interaction with your spouse over the topic of money come to the forefront of your thoughts. Is this interaction punctuated with trust or doubt? Are your conversations concerning finances outlined with generosity or control? In what ways can you and your spouse seek God's intervention to improve this area of your relationship? Write down some examples of things you would like to see done differently or managed more wisely. If nothing comes to mind, then write down some examples where you can thank and praise God for His provision in your marriage.

Prayer for Blessing and Freedom

Gracious Lord, let money not be a source of strain

in our marriage, but rather a source of celebration. Whether we lack or have an abundance, let our attitudes toward money be in agreement so that it is an area where we share the burden or the joy. Help us to encourage each other toward wise stewardship and giving. Bring us into agreement on the things where we may disagree. And show us the importance of regular communication with regard to our finances so that we are always on the same page and aware of decisions being made or needs we may have. Thank You for Your provision. Let us honor You with our choices and stewardship of all You have given to us. In Christ's name, amen.

19

Grace

Blessed are the merciful, for they will be shown mercy.

MATTHEW 5:7

Preparing Our Hearts

If you have ever gotten pulled over by a police officer, you know what the experience can do to your body. Your heart may begin to beat a bit more quickly. Sweat may start to appear at the top of your brow. Your eyes widen, and your voice softens. The presence of a police officer in the vehicle behind you with lights flashing can have a profound impact on a person in that moment of time.

If the police officer chooses to write you a ticket for whatever infraction you may have committed, the impact can carry beyond that moment. It could mean attending an online defensive driving course or appearing at the courthouse to pay your fine. If this isn't your first infraction in quite some time, it will also impact your car insurance premium rate. All of these thoughts and more generally swirl in a person's mind when a police officer stops them.

But consider what our lives would be like if God treated us according to the same or a similar set of standards. Each time we sinned, whether through lying, envying (no more social media!), or whatever the case may be, God would exact a payment to our account that we'd have to face. We'd all be in a fix before a single week was out. We could forget about getting into heaven, and even making it on earth would become impossible.

Yet God's grace covers all. His grace offered us through the death of Jesus Christ on the cross not only covered our sins, providing our entrance into heaven for eternity, but it pays the penalty of our sins for our lives on earth as well. When we sin, we go to the Father and ask forgiveness. He doesn't stand there like a stern police officer telling us that we'll still need to pay for it. No, He welcomes us with His loving arms and graciously embraces us with His spiritual blessings and favor.

How much better would each of our marriages be if the same grace the Lord shows us would be the grace we replicated and extended to our spouse? It is hypocritical to accept God's grace for sins and mistakes in your own life and then turn around and neglect to give the same grace to your spouse when he or she messes up. In Matthew 18:21-35, Jesus shares a parable concerning our lack of grace for others in light of God's grace for us, and how it affects the Father's view of us. He doesn't take it lightly when we hold others to a higher standard for our love, acceptance, kindness, and embracing than the standard He holds for us. His love is freely given because Christ created the pathway between us and Him. Likewise, our love for our spouse should be freely given, not based on merit, behavior, or a lack of messing up but rather on our spouse's identity in Christ as a person made in the very image of the God who gives all grace.

HOW MUCH BETTER
WOULD EACH OF OUR
marriages be
IF THE SAME
GRACE THE LORD
SHOWS US
WOULD BE THE GRACE
we replicated
AND EXTENDED TO
OUR SPOUSE?

The next time your spouse messes up, consider how God would go about treating you in a similar situation. If you said you were sorry, would He forgive? Or would He keep bringing it up over and over and nagging you about what you did wrong? Marriages modeled after God's own heart will reflect His peace in their homes.

Praising God

Heavenly Father, Your grace knows no boundaries. You have poured out an abundance of Your grace on us in every way. In fact, it is often so much that we grow accustomed to it and somehow even overlook it. I praise You, Lord, for the grace You embody and model for us. I worship You for Your constant flow of acceptance and forgiveness. I honor You because You are honorable in all ways, and You forgive, set aside, move on, and restore according to the mercies within You. Let our marriage be a reflection of Your grace in all ways. Help others to see Your smile in our own, and Your hope in our hearts.

Presenting the Situation

Use this portion to take the time to examine the level of grace you have shown your spouse in the past and also in the present. Has there been any change in this over the months or years? If so, what can you identify as the precursor to this change? In what ways can you increase the amount of grace you show your spouse? Are there specific things you can do so that your spouse notices a difference in this area of your marriage? Could that mean holding your tongue more and giving less judgment? Or being willing to overlook mistakes or faults that bring about challenges, while helping to focus on the solution together? Make a list of tangible things you can either do or not do to develop a deeper level of mutual grace in your marriage.

Prayer for Blessing and Freedom

Gracious Lord, let our marriage be a marriage of grace. Give us wisdom on how to start with grace in our thoughts, rather than with questioning or judgment. Show us what it means to put ourselves in the other person's shoes for that moment, and extend the kindness we would hope to receive ourselves. Let us be less critical in our words, thoughts, and assumptions, always giving the benefit of the doubt. Make trust, acceptance, and compassion the foundation of our relationship. We are a team chosen to be together by You for purposes You have called us to. Help us not to get in the way of what You want to do both in us and through us for Your glory. Make us instruments of strength and grace toward each other in every possible way. In Christ's name, amen.

20

Forgiveness

*Be kind and compassionate to one another, forgiving
each other, just as in Christ God forgave you.*

EPHESIANS 4:32

Preparing Our Hearts

A Sunday school teacher had just concluded her lesson and wanted to make sure that the kids in the room had been paying attention. So she decided to ask a follow-up question. "Can anyone explain what must happen before you can be forgiven?"

A small boy in the back of the room slowly raised his hand. Seeing no one else willing to answer, the teacher called on him. "Sin?" he replied.

The young boy had identified a truth which none of us have any issues with living out. We sin because we are human. Despite our best efforts or greatest intentions, none of us are able to live a life without sin. Scripture has made that clear, telling us that all have sinned. To expect your marriage to be a relationship that is sin free is an unrealistic expectation. No matter how loving, kind, and caring you or your spouse were to each other when you first met, dated, and married, each of you will at some point sin. Now, that doesn't mean sin has to be an ongoing practice or even all that regular, but when it does happen, responding rightly through forgiveness will help restore what sin breaks.

Forgiveness means letting the other person off of the hook for what they have done wrong and not carrying a grudge or seeking payment either through enacting a consequence or punishment of some form. Couples can enact consequences through a myriad of ways, including things such as withholding affection, intimacy, or conversation, or more overt ways such as nagging or complaining. Yet, forgiveness says that while you acknowledge the grievance done, you don't allow your emotions about that grievance to dominate your reactions and actions.

Keep in mind that forgiveness can also involve letting yourself off the hook. Too many marriages crumble through one or both spouses suffering from self-hatred, shame, or regret. This type of unforgiveness bleeds over into the relationship itself, damaging the atmosphere through negative energy and an inability to love fully. When you are unable or unwilling to love yourself, you inadvertently impact the love that flows out of you to others.

One of the first steps toward offering forgiveness involves identifying Christ's own forgiveness in your life. When you start from the mindset of His miraculous mercy, it will be much easier to extend mercy to others. Humility is the hallmark of forgiveness. Entitlement is the antithesis to forgiveness. Understanding the length God went to in order to offer an ongoing flow of forgiveness toward you ought to broaden your own capacity for offering it to your spouse.

When you choose not to forgive, you actually stand in

UNDERSTANDING
the length God went to
IN ORDER TO OFFER

AN ONGOING FLOW OF

FORGIVENESS TOWARD YOU

OUGHT TO BROADEN

YOUR OWN CAPACITY

for offering it
TO YOUR SPOUSE.

the way of God's work in your spouse's life. Consider a game of soccer. If one player makes a foul on another player, the player who made the foul will be corrected by the referee. But if the player who was fouled responds by committing his or her own foul, then the referee typically turns their attention to the one who committed the last foul. While this is a human example, the principle behind it can carry over to those times when we choose to respond to our spouse's sin with our own sin.

Not forgiving someone doesn't impact them as much as it does you. It is like choosing not to bandage or treat a wound and allowing it to worsen, become infected, and be vulnerable to further pain. Can you imagine how you would react if you had an open cut on your outer arm that you allowed to develop into an infection, and then someone unknowingly brushed up against you, opening the wound further? Your reaction to this person whose actions had been innocent toward you would be considered as an overreaction. But that's what unforgiveness does to us. When we allow it to fester in our hearts, it boils over to unsuspecting friends, family, and coworkers in ways that they do not deserve. Address the root of bitterness and the spirit of unforgiveness in your marriage before it is allowed to seep out and destroy not only your relationship as a couple, but your external relationships as well.

Praising God

Heavenly Father, thank You for the forgiveness You have freely given to me in my own life. Thank You for making the pathway to Your presence available through the death, burial, and resurrection of Jesus

Christ. Thank You that Your forgiveness comes with no strings attached and no limits. It gives me rest and peace to know that Your love is not based on my own merits, but rather is based on Your mercy. I praise and honor You for the depth, height, width, and breadth of Your love and forgiveness.

Presenting the Situation

Use this portion to think through the overall atmosphere of your marriage relationship. Is it one that carries grudges or keeps a record of wrongs? Or is it one in which forgiveness is given and the wrongs set aside, not to be brought up again? How you view wrongdoing will impact how easily you forgive your spouse. If you view it from the lens of the Lord's loving-kindness, you will be more quick to offer forgiveness. Look for ways you can shift your thinking into alignment with God's heart, especially in this ever-important area of your marriage.

_____

_____

_____

_____

_____

Prayer for Blessing and Freedom

Gracious Lord, give us a spirit of forgiveness in our marriage. Let this spirit be rooted in the confidence we both have in Your love, care, and accountability. Forgiveness is not issuing a free ticket to do wrong against each other. It is, rather, letting love lead while allowing You the freedom to develop spiritual maturity and personal growth in both of us. We trust that You will discipline where discipline is needed. We don't need to punish each other. Instead, let us be a light to the other on what kindness and love look like. More than that, increase our ability and capacity to forgive so that we do not have to carry around wounds of bitterness which will fester and bring rot to our relationship. Thank You for what You are doing both in and through us to cause us to have a marriage built on mutual love, honor, grace, and mercy. In Christ's name, amen.

21

Personal Calling

*Give her the product of her hands, and
let her works praise her in the gates.*

PROVERBS 31:31 (NASB)

Preparing Our Hearts

Not too long ago, a prominent ministry leader lost his wife suddenly to a heart attack. She was in her late thirties, and they had four children under the age of 14. He was a successful executive director of a national ministry, served on several boards, volunteered in the pro-life movement, and traveled weekly for his work. To say the demands on his schedule were high would be an understatement. A lot rode on his shoulders.

Before his wife passed away, she had built up her own ministry, which involved a magazine, nearly ten books, frequent speaking at conferences, and much more. On top of that, they had both invested in the lives of their daughters to such a degree that even their daughters served in ministry at a young age. One had starred in a Christian movie and done her own speaking and television talk-show performances.

When speaking with this husband as he reflected on his 15-year marriage, he said without hesitation, "The one thing I am grateful to say without a doubt is that I have no regrets.

RECOGNIZING THAT

both spouses have a

CALLING UNDER AND

RESPONSIBILITY TO GOD

IS KEY TO OFFERING SUPPORT,

freedom, and belief

THAT SPURS A PARTNER ON

TO FULFILL THEIR DESTINY.

I encouraged and supported my wife entirely, and because of that, she has a legacy that she left behind." This husband embraced his wife's ministry legacy, and it grew threefold under his care.

Work, careers, callings, ministries, and pursuits are often a cause of conflict in marriages because they divide time and attention away from all the other demands life seems to pile on. And yet, when they are kept in the correct mindset, they can be one of the greatest blessings a marriage experiences. This couple modeled mutual support, filling in the gaps in both schedules when the other traveled, had a writing deadline, or needed time at the office. Unfortunately, this is a rare thing in many marriages. But recognizing that both spouses have a calling under God and a responsibility to Him to fulfill that calling is key to offering the kind of support, freedom, and belief that spurs a person on to fulfill their own personal destiny. Always remember that you do not own your spouse. God does. What He desires for your spouse to accomplish ought to be accomplished. Standing in the way—whether limiting encouraging opportunities or help or adding on undue demands to their schedule—is not just standing in the way of your spouse. It is also standing in the way of what God wants done.

Take some time to examine the level of support you each provide one another in your marriage with regard to your work or personal calling. Share with each other your thoughts and feelings about this area and how you might be able to improve. Above all, pray and ask the Lord in what ways He would have you support your spouse to fully maximize his or her spiritual gifts for His glory.

Praising God

Heavenly Father, blessed is Your name forever and ever because wisdom and power belong to You. It is You who changes the times and the epochs—who removes kings and establishes kings. You raise up bosses and bring them down. You place those who are in authority over us at work in that position. We trust You as we look to You in the work we both do. It is You who reveals the profound and hidden things, giving both wisdom and knowledge. You determine our path and personal calling. You reveal it in ways we cannot always discern on our own. Open our eyes to see and know what You are doing in and through the work of our hands. Keep us occupied with the gladness of our hearts through witnessing Your blessing on our work. May our days and nights be filled with total satisfaction as You bless what we do in Your name and for Your glory. And help us to encourage each other to pursue our God-given destiny and purpose. Show us ways that we each can do this for the other. In Christ's name, amen.

Presenting the Situation

Use this portion of your prayer to the Lord to share with Him about your specific situation related to your personal callings. Whether you feel you need more freedom and support from your spouse or are the one who needs to give more, ask God to reveal these things to both of you. Pray about the ways you could show your spouse more support regarding their career and calling. It may be about how to split up household demands or meal prep more evenly. Or it may be about how to be more affirming with your words. Whatever it is, write out or simply pray about the unique aspects of supporting each other's personal calling that are present in your marriage at the moment, and then watch the Lord answer these prayers. Record the answers to your prayers in the margins or in the room provided when they occur.

_____

_____

_____

_____

_____

Prayer for Blessing and Freedom

Lord God, bless us both in our work by causing what we do to matter—not only to You but to those impacted by it and especially to us. Empower us to find satisfaction in the rewards and results of our labor because Your Word tells us this in itself is a gift from You. We ask You right now for this gift. We know work can frequently be tied to a paycheck or to producing something for someone else. It's a transaction— something we do in exchange for something we get. Help us not to get stuck in the rut of transaction. Instead, show us the significance of where You have led us to work and in what we both do. We desire so much more than clocking in and clocking out, God. We desire that You expand the borders and reach of our work and influence so that it impacts people in a profound way—whether in expanding our influence in our careers, in the office, with our coworkers, or what we produce in our homes. We no longer want to build only for someone else to inhabit, or merely plant so that someone else can eat (Isaiah 65:22-23). Wear out the work of our hands so that we will not labor in vain. Cause our work to grow and open doors for us that only You can open. Nehemiah was only a cupbearer to the king, but You used that position to lead him to rebuild his entire nation. It matters not how significant our job title or location is. What matters is what You do with it for Your glory and for others' good. In Christ's name, amen.

22

Work-Life Balance

Let the favor of the Lord our God be upon
us; and confirm for us the work of our hands;
yes, confirm the work of our hands.

PSALM 90:17 (NASB)

Preparing Our Hearts

When Moses was governing the Israelites in the wilderness, he began to experience an enormous drain on his time and mental energies. At that point, he approached his father-in-law for advice. Moses's father-in-law, Jethro, gave him some wise counsel. He suggested that Moses begin delegating the portions of his work that he could to others (Exodus 18:17-23). Now, not all issues we face in finding a healthy work-life balance arise from a lack of delegation. But what Moses's story does for us is remind us that there are often ways outside of our own thinking that can significantly help us locate that balance.

Why does a work-life balance matter? Because what you do at home as a husband, wife, or parent is just as important as what you do at work. Scripture is clear that a husband is to love his wife as Christ loved the church. That is not something a husband can do for a few minutes a day. Loving sacrificially requires time, attention, service, and personal engagement on a regular basis. Likewise, wives have

Loving sacrificially
REQUIRES TIME,
ATTENTION, SERVICE,
AND PERSONAL ENGAGEMENT
on a regular basis.

been created by God for the purpose of being a "strong help" (the Hebrew term is *ezer kenegdo*) to their husbands. That is also not something that can be done in a nonchalant manner with leftover emotions, energy, or insight.

Once you discover how to develop a biblical mindset toward marriage, you will see how important your roles at home really are. Use these guided prayers to help you in this area and watch God open doors for each other and for your home as you find new rest, new peace, and new joy.

Praising God

Heavenly Father, I praise You for the power You supply to us in our marriage that helps us see the best in each other. You have made us tools used by You to point out strengths, skills, and talents in each other. Because of Your great love and intentionality, we are able to follow that model with our spouse to both encourage and equip each other for greater service for You. After all, we can do all things through Christ who strengthens us. We can do greater works than we ever imagined because of the presence of God in us (John 14:2). But we also need to remember that this is Your word, Lord—that it is not by might nor by power but by Your Spirit that we are able to accomplish anything of worth and lasting value (Zechariah 4:6). We ask You to help us to remember this and remind us to rest. You say that You provide for those You love even while they sleep (Psalm 127:2). Make us aware that the abiding presence of Your Spirit is on us as a couple and between us in our marriage and in us as we work so that we do not strive in ways we should not. As we abide in Your presence, Your hand will grant us favor, meaning, and significance in what we do, and we will bear much fruit (John 15:8). Let us know this truth deeply so that we will be present in those moments when it doesn't seem like we are doing much, other than simply being together. Open for us Your good storehouse and give rain to our land in its season. Bless all the works of our hands. It is You who gives the power to succeed, not us (Deuteronomy 8:18). May we lend to many and not borrow. Make us the head and not the tail—above, and not underneath, as we seek to listen and obey Your commands in all we do (Deuteronomy 28:12-13). In Christ's name, amen.

Presenting the Situation

Use this portion of your prayer to the Lord to share with Him about your specific situation related to finding a healthy work and life balance. Whether you are needing to be more present in down-times or you need to let go of outcomes and trust God more with them—give these concerns to God in prayer. Pray about what concerns you the most. It could be yourself or your spouse or both of you who struggle in this area. And if you don't struggle as a couple here, thank God for that and ask for His preservation of a healthy work-life balance. Spend some time writing down specific areas you might want to see improve in this area of your marriage. Record the answers to your prayers in the margins or in the room provided when they occur.

———————————————————————————

———————————————————————————

———————————————————————————

Prayer for Blessing and Freedom

Lord God, striving for significance through what we do in our work can become a competition with other important and significant values in life. I pray that You will enable us both to find balance between work and life itself. Let our satisfaction in the fruit of our hands not drive us to get more but rather teach us to rest in what we have. Happiness and peace can be elusive while pain is all too common when our identity is tied directly to significance. Lord, we both relinquish our need for significance at the cost of personal and family peace. We do not want to experience pain or cause it as a result of any desire for significance in our work. Keep us from the pain brought about by making work an idol in itself. Reassure us of our value and significance to You in what we do. Our work is to do Your will, whether that be perceived as large or small. Whether that be cleaning the kitchen in our home, preparing a meal for our family, teaching a class, or running a business. Let us find peace in the truth of one of your servants who wrote, "There is no work better than another to please God: to pour water, to wash dishes, to be a cobbler or an apostle—all are one."[1] Help us find peace in the significance of pleasing You and serving each other in our marriage. In Christ's name, amen.

---

[1] William Tyndale

Scripture for Prayer and Meditation Related to Marriage

Psalm 37:3—Trust in the LORD and do good; dwell in the land and enjoy safe pasture.

Psalm 51:10—Create in me a pure heart, O God, and renew a steadfast spirit within me.

Romans 13:8—Let no debt remain outstanding, except the continuing debt to love one another, for whoever loves others has fulfilled the law.

1 Corinthians 13:4-7—Love is patient, love is kind. It does not envy, it does not boast, it is not proud. It does not dishonor others, it is not self-seeking, it is not easily angered, it keeps no record of wrongs. Love does not delight in evil but rejoices with the truth. It always protects, always trusts, always hopes, always perseveres.

Galatians 5:22-23—The fruit of the Spirit is love, joy, peace, forbearance, kindness, goodness,

faithfulness, gentleness and self-control. Against
such things there is no law.

1 Corinthians 13:2—If I have the gift of prophecy and
can fathom all mysteries and all knowledge, and if
I have a faith that can move mountains, but do not
have love, I am nothing.

1 Corinthians 16:14—Do everything in love.

Ephesians 4:29—Do not let any unwholesome talk come
out of your mouths, but only what is helpful for
building others up according to their needs, that it
may benefit those who listen.

Song of Songs 8:7—Many waters cannot quench love;
rivers cannot sweep it away. If one were to give
all the wealth of one's house for love, it would be
utterly scorned.

Proverbs 18:22—He who finds a wife finds what is good
and receives favor from the LORD.

Proverbs 3:3-4—Let love and faithfulness never leave you;
bind them around your neck, write them on the
tablet of your heart. Then you will win favor and a
good name in the sight of God and man.

1 John 4:16—We know and rely on the love God has for
us. God is love. Whoever lives in love lives in God,
and God in them.

Romans 15:5-6—May the God who gives endurance and encouragement give you the same attitude of mind toward each other that Christ Jesus had, so that with one mind and one voice you may glorify the God and Father of our Lord Jesus Christ.

Ephesians 4:2—Be completely humble and gentle; be patient, bearing with one another in love.

1 John 4:7—Dear friends, let us love one another, for love comes from God. Everyone who loves has been born of God and knows God.

1 Peter 4:8—Above all, love each other deeply, because love covers over a multitude of sins.

John 15:12—My command is this: Love each other as I have loved you.

2 Corinthians 12:9—He said to me, "My grace is sufficient for you, for my power is made perfect in weakness." Therefore I will boast all the more gladly about my weaknesses, so that Christ's power may rest on me.

1 Corinthians 13:13—Now these three remain: faith, hope and love. But the greatest of these is love.

Song of Songs 4:9—You have stolen my heart, my sister, my bride; you have stolen my heart with one glance of your eyes, with one jewel of your necklace.

Hebrews 10:24-25—Let us consider how we may spur one another on toward love and good deeds, not giving up meeting together, as some are in the habit of doing, but encouraging one another—and all the more as you see the Day approaching.

Proverbs 19:14—Houses and wealth are inherited from parents, but a prudent wife is from the LORD.

Proverbs 30:18-19—There are three things that are too amazing for me, four that I do not understand: the way of an eagle in the sky, the way of a snake on a rock, the way of a ship on the high seas, and the way of a man with a young woman.

1 John 4:12—No one has ever seen God; but if we love one another, God lives in us and his love is made complete in us.

Proverbs 31:10—A wife of noble character who can find? She is worth far more than rubies.

Romans 12:10—Be devoted to one another in love. Honor one another above yourselves.

Ephesians 5:21—Submit to one another out of reverence for Christ.

Deuteronomy 24:5—If a man has recently married, he must not be sent to war or have any other duty laid on him. For one year he is to be free to stay at home and bring happiness to the wife he has married.

Ephesians 4:32—Be kind and compassionate to one another, forgiving each other, just as in Christ God forgave you.

Genesis 2:18-25—The LORD God said, "It is not good for the man to be alone. I will make a helper suitable for him." Now the LORD God had formed out of the ground all the wild animals and all the birds in the sky. He brought them to the man to see what he would name them; and whatever the man called each living creature, that was its name. So the man gave names to all the livestock, the birds in the sky and all the wild animals. But for Adam no suitable helper was found. So the LORD God caused the man to fall into a deep sleep; and while he was sleeping, he took one of the man's ribs and then closed up the place with flesh. Then the LORD God made a woman from the rib he had taken out of the man, and he brought her to the man. The man said, "This is now bone of my bones and flesh of my flesh; she shall be called 'woman,' for she was taken out of man." That is why a man leaves his father and mother and is united to his wife, and they become one flesh. Adam and his wife were both naked, and they felt no shame.

Proverbs 12:4—A wife of noble character is her husband's

crown, but a disgraceful wife is like decay in his bones.

1 Peter 3:7—Husbands, in the same way be considerate as you live with your wives, and treat them with respect as the weaker partner and as heirs with you of the gracious gift of life, so that nothing will hinder your prayers.

Ephesians 5:33—However, each one of you also must love his wife as he loves himself, and the wife must respect her husband.

Song of Songs 8:6-7—Place me like a seal over your heart, like a seal on your arm; for love is as strong as death, its jealousy unyielding as the grave. It burns like blazing fire, like a mighty flame. Many waters cannot quench love; rivers cannot sweep it away. If one were to give all the wealth of one's house for love, it would be utterly scorned.

Ephesians 4:2-3—Be completely humble and gentle; be patient, bearing with one another in love. Make every effort to keep the unity of the Spirit through the bond of peace.

Proverbs 24:3-4—By wisdom a house is built, and through understanding it is established; through knowledge its rooms are filled with rare and beautiful treasures.

Colossians 3:14—Over all these virtues put on love, which binds them all together in perfect unity.

Ecclesiastes 4:9—Two are better than one, because they have a good return for their labor:

Colossians 3:19—Husbands, love your wives and do not be harsh with them.

Ephesians 5:25—Husbands, love your wives, just as Christ loved the church and gave himself up for her.

Song of Songs 4:10—How delightful is your love, my sister, my bride! How much more pleasing is your love than wine, and the fragrance of your perfume more than any spice!

Genesis 2:24—That is why a man leaves his father and mother and is united to his wife, and they become one flesh.

Ecclesiastes 4:12—Though one may be overpowered, two can defend themselves. A cord of three strands is not quickly broken.

Mark 10:9—Therefore what God has joined together, let no one separate.

1 Corinthians 7:3—The husband should fulfill his marital duty to his wife, and likewise the wife to her husband.

Ephesians 5:25-33—Husbands, love your wives, just as Christ loved the church and gave himself up for her to make her holy, cleansing her by the washing with water through the word, and to present her to himself as a radiant church, without stain or wrinkle or any other blemish, but holy and blameless. In this same way, husbands ought to love their wives as their own bodies. He who loves his wife loves himself. After all, no one ever hated their own body, but they feed and care for their body, just as Christ does the church—for we are members of his body. "For this reason a man will leave his father and mother and be united to his wife, and the two will become one flesh." This is a profound mystery—but I am talking about Christ and the church. However, each one of you also must love his wife as he loves himself, and the wife must respect her husband.